The Way to Ultimate Calm

Selected Discourses of Webu Sayadaw

The Way to Ultimate Calm

Selected Discourses of Webu Sayadaw

Translated from the Burmese by
Roger Bischoff

BPE

BPS Pariyatti Editions

BPS Pariyatti Editions
an imprint of
Pariyatti Publishing
www.pariyatti.org

Published with the consent of the original publisher.

BPS Pariyatti Editions, 2013
ISBN: 978-1681723-03-7 (Print)
Library of Congress Control Number: 2013935066

Contents

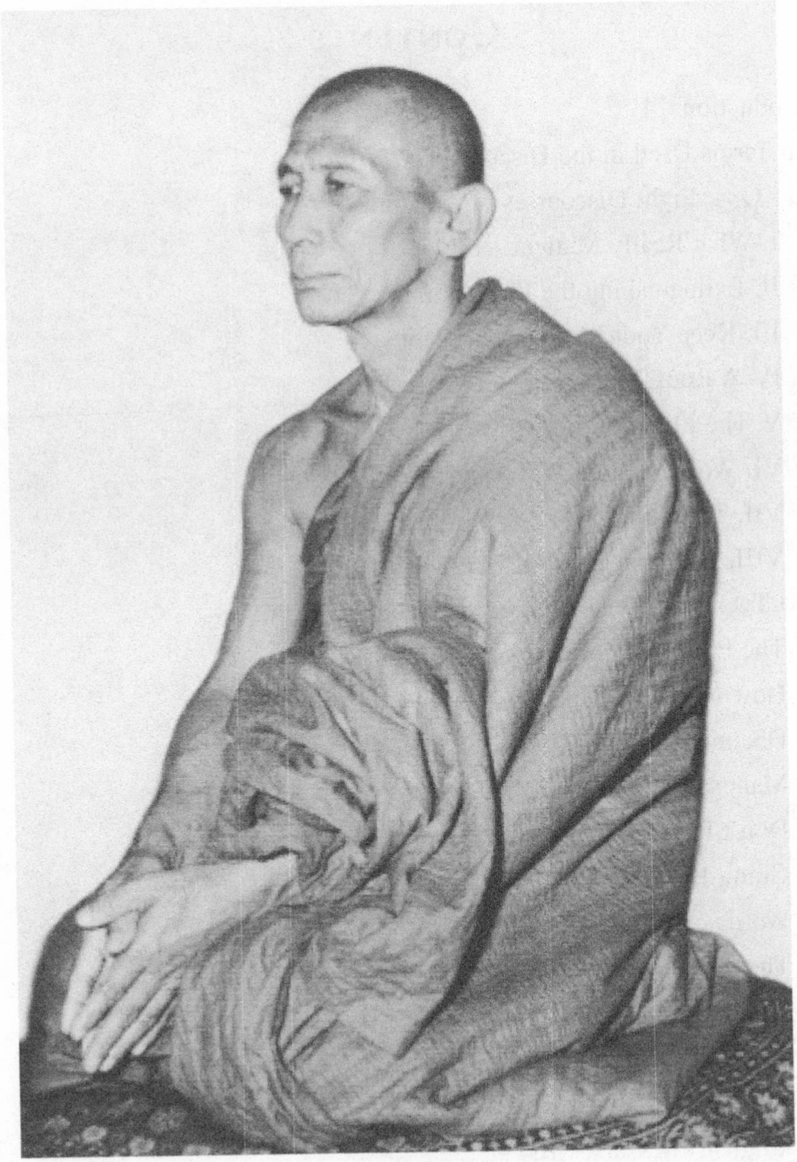

Venerable Webu Sayadaw

Introduction

Burma is one of the few countries in the world where Theravāda Buddhism still survives in its original form. The bhikkhus (monks) of Burma make every effort to preserve the Theravāda Buddhist teachings. A Buddha's Teachings deal mainly with the way the human mind works and the relationship between the mind and body. The nature of the human mind has not changed since the Buddha discovered the path leading to the understanding of the absolute truth about mind and matter. This ultimate reality and the practice leading to its realization are, and will always remain, the same, regardless of economic or social conditions, so people today who put into practice what the Buddha taught can discover this reality for themselves.

The foundation of the teachings is the Four Noble Truths: (1) the truth that all conditioned phenomena (physical and mental) are unsatisfactory (suffering), (2) the truth that there is a cause for this, (3) the truth that there is an end to this unsatisfactoriness or suffering, and (4) the truth that there is a path leading to the end of suffering.

The path to the end of suffering is called the Eightfold Noble Path as it is divided into eight parts which are grouped under the threefold training of *sīla* (morality), *samādhi* (calm control over the mind, concentration), and *paññā* (insight, wisdom).

There are actions that are called skillful (*kusala*) because they support an individual's progress towards Nibbāna, and there are unskillful (*akusala*) actions that have the contrary effect. All actions based on greed, aversion, and ignorance of the *Law of Cause and Effect* are unskillful.

The most unskillful actions are: (1) to kill a sentient being, (2) to steal, (3) to have unlawful sexual relations, (4) to speak untruth, and (5) to take intoxicants.

The Buddhist lay person undertakes to abstain from these five courses of action by taking the five moral precepts.

Once an action has been done there is no way to annul it. The effect can be minimized through the awareness of impermanence, which is the object of insight meditation. There is, however, no one, not even the Buddha, who can give an "absolution from sin", as effects are determined by the Law of *Kamma*, which is applicable to all sentient beings.

Ven. Webu Sayadaw emphasized the practice of meditation as the only way to bring the teachings of the Buddha to fulfilment. Ven. Webu

Sayadaw was believed to be an Arahat, *i.e.*, a person who has in practice understood the Four Noble Truths completely and therefore attained the end of suffering.

The technique of meditation taught by Ven. Webu Sayadaw is one of forty techniques mentioned in the scriptures for the development of *samādhi* or concentration. It is called *Ānāpāna-sati* and requires that the meditator be aware (1) that he is breathing in while he is breathing in, (2) that he is breathing out while he is breathing out, and (3) of the spot or area in the region of the nostrils where the stream of air touches while he is breathing in and out.

In the Visuddhimagga[1] Ashin Buddhaghosa describes sixteen ways of approaching Ānāpāna meditation, but Ven. Webu Sayadaw kept reminding his disciples that they did not need to know about all of these, all they really needed to know was the reality of in- and out-breathing.

Though Ānāpāna is a way of developing *samatha* (tranquillity of mind), *samādhi* (concentration of mind to one-pointedness) and *jhāna* (absorption states), Ven. Webu Sayadaw said that when concentration is developed to a sufficient degree, the meditator automatically gains insight into the three characteristics of nature — *anicca, dukkha,* and *anattā* — if his mind is open to recognize them. *Anicca* means "impermanence" or "instability", "change", and is characteristic of all conditioned phenomena, be they physical or mental. *Dukkha* denotes the unsatisfactory nature of all these phenomena: nothing that is impermanent or changing can ever give lasting satisfaction. *Anattā* means "non-self", "non-soul", and applies to all phenomena — conditioned and unconditioned. According to the Buddha, there is no permanent ego, soul, or personal entity, but only physical and mental phenomena interrelating. In Buddhism the understanding of these three characteristics of *anicca, dukkha,* and *anattā* is called *paññā* or wisdom, and *paññā* is the quality which enables a meditator to reach Nibbāna.

U Hte Hlain, the collector of some of the discourses contained in this book, writes, "Ven. Webu Sayadaw preached sometimes five, sometimes ten times a day. Seven main points were always included in his discourses. If Ven. Webu Sayadaw gave 10,000 discourses in his life, then these points were expounded by him 10,000 times. He always included them, even if he had to repeat them again and again. He always explained the teachings in simple terms, so that the ordinary person could understand. He tried to explain the Dhamma in such a way that the most difficult thing became easy."

The seven Points are:

(1) One can only expect the fulfilment of one's aspirations if one is perfect in morality.
(2) When practising generosity (*dāna*) in the religion of the Buddha, the mental attitude and volition involved are very important.
(3) Believing in the *law of cause and effect* one should always act with an upright mind.
(4) One should not aspire to any happiness of either the human or celestial worlds — which are impermanent — but only to Nibbāna.
(5) Because of the arising of the Buddha we have the opportunity to practise right conduct (*caraṇa*) and wisdom (*paññā*) fully and therefore benefit greatly.
(6) From the moment we are born to the moment we die, there is the in-breath and the out-breath. This is easy for everybody to understand. Every time we breathe in or out, the breath touches near the nostrils. Every time it touches we should be aware of it.
(7) While we are walking, working, doing anything, we should always be aware of the in- and out-breath.

Paramount importance is given to right action and the experience and understanding drawn from it. As we shall see in the discourses, Ven. Webu Sayadaw wants his audience to realize the teachings through their own experience, for themselves, rather than through hearing them; and he says that in this way, as they begin to see the teachings as a reality, people can pass beyond doubt.

Ven. Webu Sayadaw was born on the sixth day of the waxing moon of Tabaung of the year 1257 (Burmese Era) (February 17, 1896) in Ingyinbin, a small village near Shwebo in upper Burma. He was ordained as a novice at the age of nine and was given the name Shin Kumara. All boys in Buddhist Burma become novices at their local monastery at some time in their teens or even earlier, but usually return home after a predetermined span of time. Shin Kumara, however, decided to stay at the monastery to receive a religious education. At the age of twenty, he was ordained as a full member of the Saṅgha, the Buddhist order of monks, receiving the *Upasampadā* ordination, and was thereafter addressed as U Kumara.[2]

U Kumara went to Mandalay to study at the famous Masoyein monastery, the leading monastic university of the time. In the seventh year after his full ordination, he abandoned the study of the Pāḷi scriptures and left the monastery to put into practice what he had learned about meditation.

Buddhist monks can choose between two activities: the study of the scriptures (*pariyatti*), or the practice of Buddhist meditation (*paṭipatti*). While scholarly monks tend to live in centres of learning in order to be able to pass on their knowledge to younger monks, meditating monks leave the busy atmosphere of the monasteries to retire to a solitary life in the jungle. They often live in caves or simply under trees and come into contact with people only on the occasion of their morning alms-rounds.

After leaving the Masoyein monastery in Mandalay at the age of twenty-seven, U Kumara spent four years in solitude. Then he went to his native village of Ingyinbin for a brief visit. His former teacher at the village monastery requested U Kumara to teach him the technique of meditation he had adopted, and U Kumara did so. "This is a shortcut to Nibbāna," he said, "anyone can use it. It stands up to investigation and is in accordance with the teachings of the Buddha as conserved in the scriptures. It is the straight path to Nibbāna."

There is a set of thirteen practices called the *dhutaṅga*[3] that are often taken up by monks living in solitude. They are designed to combat laziness and indulgence. One of these practices is never to lie down, not even to sleep. Monks taking up this particular practice spend the nights sitting and meditating or walking and meditating to rid themselves of sleepiness. The thirteen *dhutaṅga* may be taken up individually or together.

Ven. Webu Sayadaw is said to have followed this practice of never lying down all his life. He taught that effort was the key to success, not only in worldly undertakings, but also in meditation, and that sleeping was a waste of time. I was told by one of his disciples that on the occasion of his ordination under Ven. Webu Sayadaw, he had a mosquito net and a pillow, in addition to the monks requisites. Ven. Webu Sayadaw, pointing at them, asked him what they were. "A pillow and a mosquito net, sir." "Are these part of the monks requisites?"[4] "No, sir." And the newly ordained monk decided to give these "luxuries" back to his family.

Ven. Webu Sayadaw undertook pilgrimages to the Buddhist sites of India and of Ceylon. He passed away on June 26, 1977, in the meditation centre at Ingyinbin, his native village.

The Setting

Most of these discourses were given before large audiences during Ven. Webu Sayadaw's travels in lower Burma. The person or persons answering Ven. Webu Sayadaw are lay-people sitting up front and close to him.

Some of the discourses are translated from a collection of discourses collected and introduced by U Hte Hlain and published by the Ministry of

Religious Affairs of Burma. Others have been transcribed from tape by the translator and then rendered in English.

Because they were delivered extemporaneously, the discourses are repetitive and were edited slightly so that they lend themselves better to reading. Care was taken, however, to edit only obvious repetitions and only when they had merely rhetorical value. The reader may still find the discourses repetitive, but with some patience and "mindfulness" he will discover in them many insights into practical Buddhism.

Ven. Webu Sayadaw's discourses are not meant for the person who prefers the study of Buddhist philosophy to the practice. His refreshing simplicity, his patience, his lovely sense of humour, and his humility —are revealed in the dialogues with his audience. Moreover, the statements of the people in the audience offer us a glimpse of how Buddhism is practised in Burma today.

Pāḷi Terms Used in the Discourses

To understand the discourses, the reader should be familiar with some basic teachings of Buddhism. Neither the explanations given nor the points selected for explanation attempt to give a complete picture of the teachings of the Buddha, but they should enable the reader to understand the discourses included in this collection.

The Theravāda Buddhist scriptures can be divided into "Three (*ti*) Baskets (*piṭaka*)" and are therefore called the *Tipiṭaka* in Pāḷi, the language in which they were originally written down.

The three baskets are:

(1) Vinaya-piṭaka: The books of monastic discipline.

(2) Suttanta-piṭaka: The books of discourses of the Buddha and his major disciples.

(3) Abhidhamma-piṭaka: the books of ultimate truths; an analysis of physical and mental phenomena into their ultimate components.

Scholarly training (*pariyatti*) in Theravāda Buddhism consists of the study of these scriptures. Practical training (*paṭipatti*), with which these discourses mainly deal, is concerned with the practice of *sīla* (morality), *samādhi* (concentration) and *paññā* (insight) and culminates in the attaining of the four stages of Nibbāna (*paṭivedha*).

The word Dhamma can have many different meanings, but in the context of these discourses it is always used to mean the teachings of the Buddha.

Sīla

For the monks, the training in morality consists of the observance of 227 rules. The collection of these rules is called the Pātimokkha and is part of the Vinaya.

Lay-people have to observe five or eight rules of training: the five *sīlas* (*pañca-sīla*), or the eight *sīlas* (*Uposatha-sīla*).

Pañca-sīla:

(1) to abstain from killing any living being;

(2) to abstain from taking what is not given;

(3) to abstain from sexual misconduct;

(4) to abstain from telling untruths;

(5) to abstain from intoxicating drink and drugs.

Uposatha-sīla:

(1) to (5) as above;

(6) to abstain from eating solid food after midday;

(7) to abstain from dancing, singing, music, and watching unseemly shows; from the use of garlands, perfumes, and unguents; and from things that tend to beautify and adorn;

(8) to abstain from high and luxurious seats and beds.

The field of *sīla* is, of course, much wider. These precepts are but the absolute basics of Right Conduct (*caraṇa*) a Buddhist lay-person is expected to observe. The purpose of *sīla* or *caraṇa* is to bring physical and verbal action under control.

Samādhi

Tranquil concentration of the mind and control over the mind. The Buddha taught forty techniques to achieve *samādhi*, of which Ānāpāna is one. The Buddha taught that *sīla* is a prerequisite for *samādhi*.

Paññā

Paññā, the understanding through personal experience of the characteristics which the Buddha said were in the nature of all conditioned things, *i.e.*, *anicca* (impermanence), *dukkha* (unsatisfactoriness), and *anattā* (absence of a permanent personal entity such as an ego, self or soul), is achieved through Vipassanā meditation. In Vipassanā meditation the mind is set to a perfect state of balance, and then the mind's attention is projected to the changing nature (*anicca*), or the unsatisfactory nature (*dukkha*), or the impersonal nature (*anattā*) of all physical and mental phenomena encountered.

Sīla, *samādhi*, and *paññā* are called the three *sikkhās*, the threefold training. In addition to this threefold division, we often also find a twofold one: (1) *caraṇa*: right conduct (*sīla*) and (2) *bhāvanā*: mental development (*samādhi* and *paññā*). Another method of enumeration is (1) *dāna* (generosity, otherwise included in *sīla*); (2) *sīla*, and (3) *bhāvanā*.

What are normally called beings, *i.e.*, Devas, Brahmās, humans, animals, etc., are seen in Buddhism as nothing but a combination and continuous arising and dissolution of mental and physical phenomena. "Mind" in Pāḷi is *nāma* and "matter", *rūpa*.

Mind and matter (*nāma* and *rūpa*) are both impermanent or unstable. "But in expounding the theory of *anicca*, the Buddha started with the behavior that makes matter, and matter as known to the Buddha is very much smaller than the atom that science of today has discovered. The Buddha made it known to his disciples that everything that exists, be it animate or inanimate, is composed of *kalāpas* (very much smaller than atoms), each dying out simultaneously as it becomes. Each *kalāpa* is a mass formed of the eight nature elements, namely, solidity, liquidity, heat, motion, color, odor, taste, and nutriment. The first four are called material qualities which are predominant in a *kalāpa*. The other four are merely subsidiaries that are dependent upon and born out of the former. A *kalāpa* is the minutest particle in the physical plane — still beyond the range of science today.

"It is only when the eight nature elements (which have merely the characteristic of behavior) are together that the entity of a *kalāpa* is formed. In other words, the co-existence for a moment of these eight nature elements of behavior makes a mass, just for a moment, which in Buddhism is known as a *kalāpa*."[5] A being is also defined as the coming together of the five aggregates (*pañca khandha*). In this case, one aggregate is *rūpa* or matter, while *nāma* or mind is divided into four aggregates: (1) *viññāna*, consciousness, (2) *saññā*, perception or recognition, (3) *vedanā*, sensation, feeling, (4) *saṅkhāra*, force of past action. (It can be seen from this that the term *nāma* is wider than the English term "mind.")

Saṅkhāra (or *kamma* in popular terminology) is the force left behind by actions in the past, the "past" meaning here billions and billions of lives in *saṃsāra*, the cycle of births and deaths. *Saṅkhāra* is a cause for the experience of sense impressions.

There are three possible ways of reacting to a sensory contact or sense impression: *kusala* (skilful reaction), *akusala* (unskilful reaction), and *avyakata* (neutral reaction). Practically speaking, neutral reaction is possible only for an *Arahat*, *i.e.*, for someone who experiences no wanting (*lobha*) or dislike (*dosa*) and whose mind is not clouded by any form of delusion (*moha*) about the Four Noble Truths as taught by the Buddha. Every intelligent ordinary being, however, is capable of *kusala* rather than *akusala* reactions. In order to be able to react skillfully, one has to have control not only over one's physical and verbal actions, but also over one's mind. Every physical and verbal action begins in the mind, and the action that results in *saṅkhāra* or *kamma* is the mental volition accompanying this physical and verbal action.

Initially, Ānāpāna meditation is but a tool to concentrate and calm the mind. At this stage no attention is given to sensations, thoughts, emotions, and similar mental phenomena. The attention of the mind is meant to stay with the simple awareness of the physical touch of air brushing over the skin below the nose, above the upper lip. In this case the three unwholesome roots, *i.e.*, *lobha* (greed), *dosa* (anger, aversion), and *moha* (delusion), are held in abeyance, and what is left are the Three Wholesome Roots: *alobha* (non-greed), *adosa* (non-anger), and *amoha* (knowledge, understanding).

This momentary concentration of the mind on physical phenomena results in a temporary mental purity which in Buddhism is called *samādhi*.

To come to a lasting purity of mind, according to Buddhism, matter and mental aggregates have to be observed in the light of their constant change (*anicca*), their unsatisfactoriness (*dukkha*), and the absence of an "I", a lasting personality or soul (*anattā*). By experiencing these characteristics, or indeed, any one characteristic, a person can attain freedom from all attachment, and thus reach the end of suffering.

The Four Noble Truths

The Four Noble Truths so often referred to in the discourses are the following:

(1) The Truth of Suffering (*dukkha*),
(2) The Truth of the Origin of Suffering (*samudaya*),
(3) The Truth of the Cessation of Suffering (*nirodha*)
(4) The Truth of the Path leading to the Cessation of Suffering (*magga*).

The term *dukkha* is traditionally translated as "suffering" (and is the same term we rendered as "unsatisfactoriness" above). The Noble Truth of Suffering states that all conditioned states are unsatisfactory or connected with suffering. The Noble Truth of the Origin of Suffering declares the origin of suffering as being craving (*lobha*). The Noble Truth of the Cessation of Suffering teaches that suffering ceases as soon as all craving ceases. The Noble Truth of the Path Leading to the Cessation of Suffering gives us the Noble Eightfold Path which consists of eight limbs arranged in three groups: *sīla*, *samādhi*, and *paññā*.

Sīla:	*sammā-vācā*	Right speech
	sammā-kammanta	Right action
	sammā-ajīva	Right livelihood
Samādhi:	*sammā-vāyāma*	Right effort
	sammā-sati	Right attentiveness
	sammā-samādhi	Right concentration
Paññā:	*sammā-diṭṭhi*	Right view
	sammā-saṅkappa	Right thinking

The Thirty-One Planes of Existence

The Buddha taught that the universe is composed of innumerable world systems and each world system in turn is composed of thirty-one planes of existence.

These are:

Four *arūpa* planes of Brahmās (these planes, where mind but no matter exists, are attained through the highest absorption states, *jhāna*).
Sixteen Fine-material planes of Brahmās (attained through absorption states).
Six Deva planes (attained through the practice of *sīla* and of generosity).
The human plane (attained through the practice of *sīla* and of generosity).
Four Lower planes: Animals, Ghosts, Demons, Hell (attained through bad deeds).

The thirty-one planes of existence are divided into three spheres (*loka*) the *arūpa-loka*, which consists of the four highest Brahmā planes; the *rūpa-loka*, which consists of the remaining sixteen Brahmā planes; and the *kāma-loka*, which is the sphere of sensual desires (*kāma*) and includes the four lower planes, the human plane and the six Deva planes.

Beings are reborn in the different planes according to the mental action or *kamma* created at the moment of death (*cuti*). A good, pure mental action gives rise to a being in the human or Deva planes. The practice of the absorption states (*jhāna*) leads to rebirth in the Brahmā planes. If, at the moment of death, the mind is impure, *i.e.*, inclined towards anger, greed, delusion, the force produced by this impure mind will result in rebirth in one of the four lower planes of existence.

In Buddhism the training of the mind is deemed of paramount importance: if a person has achieved control over the mind, he can keep the mind focused and calm even if unpleasant states of mind arise and can thus approach death with confidence.

The Four Stages of Nibbāna

To attain the pure state of Nibbāna, the end of all suffering, an individual has to free himself of the ten fetters that tie him to conditioned existence. This process of liberation comes about in a sequence of four stages.

The ten fetters are: (1) belief in the existence of a permanent ego, self or soul, (2) doubts about the Eightfold Noble Path and the Four Noble Truths, (3) attachment to rites and rituals, (4) sensual desire, (5) anger and aversion, (6) craving for fine material existence, (7) craving for non-material existence, (8) pride, (9) agitation, and (10) incomplete understanding of the Four Noble Truths.

The four stages are:

(I) *Sotāpatti* (stream-entry): An individual is freed of the first three of the ten fetters that tie beings to the round of birth and death: (1) belief in the existence of a permanent ego [self or soul], (2) doubts about the Eightfold Noble Path and the Four Noble Truths, and (3) attachment to rites and rituals.

(II) *Sakadagāmī* (once-returner): An individual attenuates the fetters of (4) sensual desire and (5) anger.

(III) *Anāgāmī* (non-returner): An individual is freed completely from (4) sensual desire and (5) anger and ill-will.

(IV) *Arahat*: An individual is freed completely of the remaining fetters of, (6) craving for fine-material existence, (7) craving for non-material existence, (8) pride, (9) agitation, and (10) incomplete understanding of the Four Noble Truths.

Each one of the four stages is attained through a Path Stage (*magga*) and a Fruition Stage (*phala*). These are technical terms, but are popularly used in Burma as synonyms for Nibbāna. Persons who have attained to one of these four stages are known as *Ariyas*, Noble Ones. These stages can only be attained through Vipassanā (insight) meditation.

The Ten Pāramīs

The ten *pāramīs* are a set of ten qualities in which an individual has to perfect himself in order to be able to attain Nibbāna.

The ten *pāramīs* are :

(1) Charity	(*dāna*)
(2) Morality	(*sīla*)
(3) Renunciation	(*nekkhamma*)
(4) Understanding	(*paññā*)
(5) Effort	(*viriya*)
(6) Patience	(*khanti*)
(7) Truthfulness	(*sacca*)
(8) Determination	(*adhiṭṭhāna*)
(9) Loving Kindness	(*mettā*)
(10) Equanimity	(*upekkhā*)

With the help of the introduction, it should not be difficult to understand the discourses. Special care was taken not to use Pāḷi terms except those that are used so often that it seemed wiser if the reader integrated them into his vocabulary; I mean terms such as *sīla*, *samādhi*, etc. At the end of the book the reader will find an index of Pāḷi words to refresh his memory. The Pāḷi terms that are commonly used in Burma and generally not translated into the Burmese vernacular are given and explained in endnotes for the interested reader.

I would like to add that there is no necessity for the reader to understand the philosophical underpinnings of Buddhism before reading these discourses; he should rather try to keep his mind open to the profound simplicity and sincerity that are the characteristics of the speaker and his words.

Many of the explanations in this introduction are drawn from the booklet *Dhamma Texts by Sayagyi U Ba Khin* (Sayagyi U Ba Khin Memorial Trust, U.K., Dhamma Texts Series 1, 1985; revised ed., 1991).

Roger B

Part One

Eight Discourses on Dhamma

Discourse One

What Really Matters

Ven. Webu Sayadaw: You have taken up moral conduct (*sīla*). Now that you have undertaken to perfect yourselves in the perfection of morality (*sīla-pāramī*), fulfil it to the utmost. Only if you fulfil *sīla* to the utmost will all your aspirations be met. You will be happy now and in the future.

Only the teachings of the Buddha can give you real happiness—in the present and in the remainder of *saṃsāra.*[1] The teachings of the Buddha are enshrined in the Three Collections, or the canonical Tipiṭaka.[2] The Tipiṭaka is very extensive. If we take the essence out of the Tipiṭaka we shall find the thirty-seven Factors of Awakening (*bodhipakkhiyādhammā*)?[3] The essence of the thirty-seven Factors of Awakening is the eight constituents of the Noble Eightfold Path (*maggaṅgas*). The essence of the Noble Eightfold Path is the threefold training (*sikkhā*): higher morality, higher mindfulness, and higher wisdom (*adhisīla, adhicitta, adhipaññā*). The essence of the threefold training is the unique Universal Law (*eko dhammo*).[4]

If your body and mind are under control, as they are now, there can be no roughness of physical or verbal action. This is *adhisīla* or perfect morality.

If *adhisīla* becomes strong, the mind will become peaceful and tranquil and lose its harshness. This is called *adhicitta.*[5]

If *adhicitta* (*samādhi*) becomes strong and the mind stays one-pointed for a long period, then you will realize that in a split second matter arises and dissolves billions and billions of times. If mind (*nāma*) knows matter (*rūpa*), it knows that matter becomes and disintegrates billions and billions of times in the wink of an eye.[6] This knowledge of arising and disintegration is called *adhipaññā*.

Whenever we breathe in or out, the in-coming and the out-going air touches somewhere in or near the nostrils. The sensitive matter (*kāya-pasāda*) registers the touch of *air.*[7] In this process, the entities touching are matter, and the entity knowing the touch is mind. So do not go around asking others about mind and matter, observe your breathing and you will find out about them for yourselves.

When the air comes in, it will touch. When the air goes out, it will touch. If you know this touch continuously, then wanting (*lobha*), dislike (*dosa*), and delusion (*moha*) do not have the opportunity to arise, and the fires of greed, anger, and delusion will subside.

You cannot know the touch of air before it actually occurs. After it has gone, you cannot know it any more. Only while the air moves in or out can you feel the sensation of touch. This we call the present moment.

While we feel the touch of air, we know that there are only mind and matter. We know for ourselves that there is no "I," no other person, no man and woman, and we realize for ourselves that what the Buddha said is indeed true. We needn't ask others. While we know in-breath and out-breath, there is no I or *attā*.[8]

When we know this, our view is pure; it is right view. We know in that moment that there is nothing but *nāma* and *rūpa*, mind and matter. We also know that mind and matter are two different entities. If we thus know how to distinguish between *nāma* and *rūpa*, we have attained the ability to distinguish between mind and matter (*nāma-rūpa-pariccheda-ñāṇa*).

If we know the touch of air as and when it occurs, our mind is pure and we get the benefits thereof. Do not think that the benefits you get thus, even in a split second, are few. Do not think that those who meditate do not get any advantages from their practice. Now that you are born in a happy plane and encounter the teachings of a Buddha, you can obtain great benefits. Do not worry about eating and drinking, but make all the effort you can.

SAYADAW: Is this present time not auspicious?

DISCIPLE: Yes sir, it is.

S: Yes, indeed! Can't those good people attain their aspiration to Nibbāna who, with an open mind, receive and practice the teachings of the Buddha, just like the noble people of the past who received the instructions from the Buddha himself?

D: Yes sir, they can.

S: So, how long does the Buddha's Sāsana (teaching) last?[9]

D: For five thousand years, sir.

S: And now tell me, how many of these five thousand years have passed?

D: Sir, about half this time span has gone.

S: So, how much remains still?

D: About two thousand five hundred years, sir.

S: What is the life span of a human being now?[10]

D: About one hundred years, sir.

S: How old are you?

D: I am thirty-seven years old, sir.

S: So, how much longer do you have to live?

D: Sixty-three years, sir.

S: But can you be sure that you will live that long?

D: That I don't know, sir.

S: You don't know yourself how long you are going to live?

D: No, sir, it isn't possible to know this for sure.

S: But even as we are born we can be sure to have to suffer old age, disease, and death.

D: Yes, sir.

S: Can we request old age, pain, and death to desist for some time, to go away for some time?

D: No, sir.

S: No, they never rest. Can we ask them to stop their work?

D: No, sir, we cannot.

S: In that case we can be certain that we have to die?

D: Yes, sir, it is certain that we all have to die.

S: It is certain that all have to die. What about living?

D: We can't be sure how long we have left to live, sir.

S: Someone whose life span is thirty years dies when the thirty years are up. If your life span is forty or fifty years, you will die when you are forty or fifty years old. Once someone is dead, can we get him back?

D: No, sir, we can't.

S: However many years of your life have passed, they have passed. What is it that you have not accomplished yet?

D: The happiness of the Paths and Fruition States, Nibbāna.

S: Yes, inasmuch as you haven't attained the Paths and Fruition States yet, you have been defeated. Have you used the years that have passed well or have you wasted your time?

D: I have wasted my time, sir.

S: Then do not waste the time that you have got left. This time is there for you to strive steadfastly with energy. You can be sure that you will die, but you can't be sure how much longer you have got to live. Some live very long. Venerable Mahā-Kassapa and Venerable Mahā-Kaccāyana lived to over one hundred years of age. Some live for eighty years. To be able to live that long we have to be full of respect for those who deserve respect, and we have to be very humble. Do you pay respects to your father and mother?

D: We do, sir.

S: Do you pay respects to people who are older than you or of a higher standing than you?

D: We do pay respects to people who are older than us or are holding a higher position than we do. Even if someone is just one day older or even just half a day older, we pay respects, sir.

S: When do you pay respects to them?

D: At night, before we go to bed, we pay respects to the Buddha, and at that time we also pay respects to our seniors.

S: What about other times?

D: At other times we do not pay respects, sir.

S: You say that you pay respects to your seniors after you have paid respects to the Buddha. But do you show respect to those who live with you and to those who are of the same age? If I were to put parcels of money worth $1000 each along the road for anyone to take, would you fellows take one?

D: Of course we would, sir.

S: And if you found a second one, would you take that too?

D: Of course we would, sir.

S: And if you found a third bundle of bank notes, would you take that as well?

D: We would take it, of course, sir.

S: After having got one, wouldn't you want someone else to have one?

D: We wouldn't think that way, sir.

S: If you happened to be with a friend, would you let him find one bundle of notes thinking, "I shall pretend not to see that one. After all, I have one already"? Would you let him have one or would you grab them all and run for it?

D: I would grab all I could get and run for it, sir.

S: Yes, yes, you fellows are not very pleasant. When it comes to money, you are unable to give to anyone. But then you say that you are respectful and humble just because you pay respects to the Buddha in the evenings. If you cherish thoughts such as, "Why is he better off than I am? Is his understanding greater than mine?," then your mind is still full of pride. If you pay respects to your parents and teachers, to those older, wiser, or of higher standing, without pride, then you will live to more than one hundred years. If you show respect to such people, will you get only $1000? Will you get only money?

D: It will be more than just money.

S: Yes, indeed! And though you know what really matters, you wouldn't even give $1000 to someone else, but would rather run and get it for yourselves. When the Buddha, out of compassion, taught the Dhamma, did everybody understand it?

D: No, sir, not everyone understood it.

S: Why is this so?

D: Some didn't listen to the Buddha, sir.

S: Only if you take the teachings of the Buddha for yourselves can you attain *sammā-sam-bodhi* (Buddhahood), *pacceka-bodhi* (Pacceka-Buddhahood), *agga-sāvaka-bodhi* (chief-discipleship), *mahā-sāvaka-bodhi* (leading-discipleship), *pakati-sāvaka-bodhi* (Arahatship). If you want to attain one of these forms of awakening, you can. Through the teachings of the Buddha you can attain happiness now, a happiness that will stay with you also in the future.

How long does it take for a paddy seed to sprout?

D: Only overnight, sir.

S: It takes only a day for it to sprout. Now, if you keep the seed, a good quality seed of course, after sprouting and do not plant it, will it grow?

D: No, sir, it won't.

S: Even though you have a good quality seed, if you do not plant it, it will not grow. It is just the same with the teachings of the Buddha; only if you accept them will you understand them. If you learn how to live with the awareness of mind and matter arising, what do you achieve ?

D: This awareness is called *vijjā* sir.

S: If one lives without the teachings of the Buddha, what do you call that?

D: That is *avijjā*, sir, ignorance.

S: If you live all your life with *vijjā*, understanding of the Buddha-Dhamma, then where will you go after death?

D: To some good existence, sir.

S: What will happen after a life full of ignorance?

D: One will go to the lower realms, sir.

S: Now, say an old man about seventy years old is paying respects to the Buddha. While doing so, he cannot keep his mind focused on the Dhamma, but he allows it to wander here and there. If this old man dies at that moment, where will he be reborn?

D: He will go to the lower worlds, sir.

S: Really? Think carefully before you answer. He is paying respects to the Buddha, and he is meditating. So, where will he go if he dies at that moment?

D: He will go to the lower worlds, sir.

S: But why?

D: Because his mind is wandering all over, sir.

S: Yes. What are the qualities arising in the mind of a person living in ignorance?

D: They are greed (*lobha*), aversion (*dosa*), and delusion (*moha*).[11]

S: What is *lobha*?

D: *Lobha* is to want something, sir.

S: *Lobha* includes any liking, being attracted by something, wanting. One who dies with any liking or wanting in his mind is said to be reborn as a ghost.

But what is *dosa*?

D: *Dosa* is enmity, sir.

S: Yes, *dosa* is the cause for your fighting. *Dosa* arises because you do not get what you want and what you get you don't want. Dislike is *dosa*. If you die with dislike in your mind, you are reborn in hell. *Moha* is ignorance about benefits derived from being charitable, being moral and practicing meditation. If you die with delusion in your mind, you will be reborn as an animal. Nobody, no god, no *deva* or *brahmā* has created body and mind. They are subject to the law of nature, to arising and dissolution, just as the Buddha taught. If a person dies concentrating on the awareness of mind and matter and knowing about arising and dissolution of these, then, according to the teaching of the Buddha, he will be reborn as a man, *deva*, or *brahmā*. If someone is going where he wants to go, does he need to ask others for the way?

D: No, sir.

S: Does one have to ask others, "Do I live with knowledge or in ignorance"?

D: No, sir.

S: No. Indeed not. Therefore, work hard to bring the perfections (*pāramī*) you have accumulated in the whole of *saṃsāra* to fruition. Be steadfast in your effort.

Act as the wise people of the past did after receiving the teachings directly from the Buddha; they worked for Nibbāna. Knowing that you too have been born in a favourable plane of existence, nothing can stop you from working up to the attainment of the eight stages of Nibbāna.

Practice with strong effort and with steadfastness, and make sure that not even a little time is wasted. Advise and urge others to practice too. Strive with happiness in your heart and when you are successful, be truly happy.

Discourse Two

Extinguishing the Fires Within

WEBU SAYADAW: There are duties towards the pagoda compound (*cetiyaṅgaṇa*)[12] and the Bodhi tree compound (*bodhiyaṅgaṇa*),[13] towards one's teachers, parents, wife, and children. If we fulfil these duties, we practice good conduct (*caraṇa*), and this is virtue (*sīla*).

While we are fulfilling our duties, is it not possible to practice mindfulness of breathing too? If we do not fulfil these duties, can we say that our *sīla* is complete? If our *sīla* is not perfect, can we expect to experience the happiness we aspire for? If we are not happy, if we can't get good concentration, and if our mind is not concentrated, we can't attain insight wisdom (*paññā*).

> [Ven. Webu Sayadaw assembled the monks in the ordination hall to recite the 227 monks' rules (the Pātimokkha) and to attend to other matters of the community. At the completion of this meeting, he used to give a discourse to the lay people present.]

SAYADAW: Today is the Uposatha day.[14] At dawn you all got up with the thought, "Today is the Uposatha day," and you undertook to keep the eight precepts. Have you been mindful continuously since then?

DISCIPLE: No, sir, we haven't.

S: How much of this time have you spent being aware of in-breath and out-breath?

D: At times we are aware, at times we are not, sir.

S: How long did your mind stay with the object and how much time did you lose?

D: (No reply.)

S: As you remain silent, I assume that you have been able to keep up your awareness all the time.

D: No, sir, we haven't.

S: In that case I have to ask you some more questions. How many times does your mind dissolve in a flash of lightning?

D: Billions and billions of times, sir.

S: So it arises and disintegrates billions of times. Every time the mind arises it takes some object, pleasant or unpleasant, liked or disliked. Is there a time when this constant, continuous stream of mental objects is cut or interrupted?

D: No, sir, the mind always takes an object.

S: Yes, and these good and bad friends arise in your mind due to the skilful and unskilful deeds or *kamma* you have done in the past. Now, if a pleasant object, which we call a good friend, enters the stream of consciousness, what happens?

D: Liking or *lobha* arises, sir.

S: If liking arises, is this good or bad?

D: It is bad (*akusala*), sir.

S: But if a bad friend, an unpleasant mind-object arises, what happens then?

D: Dislike or *dosa* arises, sir.

S: If we allow dislike to arise, are we skilful or unskilful? Is this action *kusala* or *akusala*?

D: It is unskilful, sir.

S: So, if we accept the agreeable mind-objects, liking, craving, wanting, and lust arise, and we are creating unskilful acts which lead to the four lower planes of existence. But if unpleasant thoughts or images arise and we take possession of them, then worry, grief, suffering, anger, and aversion arise, and these mental states lead to the lower planes too. Now, when is the time at which no pleasant or unpleasant thought or image or sound or sight or taste or touch arises?

D: There is no such time, sir. The mind always takes an object.

S: And all these objects arising in our minds are the results of the deeds we have done in the past, in *saṃsāra*. If an object is pleasant or unpleasant, when it arises what do you normally do?

D: We react unskilfully and create *akusala-kamma* for ourselves, sir.

S: If a pleasant object arises in the mind, liking, craving, wanting arise. This craving, this *lobha*, what is it like? Is it not like a fire? *Lobha* is like a fire. What about *dosa*, disliking, aversion, and hatred?

D: *Dosa* is also like a fire, sir.

S: So, whatever arises, we have to suffer the burning of fire, don't we?

D: Yes, sir.

S: But, of course, if *lobha* and *dosa* have to arise, let them arise. If we are practicing the teachings of the Buddha, can they affect us? While we are practicing Ānāpāna meditation, lobha and dosa don't get an opportunity to possess our minds.

The teachings of the Buddha resemble the great lake Anottata.[15] If the fires of *lobha* or *dosa* or any other fires fall into this lake, they are extinguished, and we don't have to suffer their scorching heat any longer. Only if we know each arising of the mind in the billions of times it arises in a split second, can we justly say that we have achieved *adhipaññā*, real wisdom and insight.

Mind and body arise billions of times in the wink of an eye, and with it your good and bad friends. If you are not watchful, these good and bad deeds of yours will again be accumulated in you billions of times. Now, who is responsible for the pleasant and unpleasant sensations that continuously arise in your body?

D: We ourselves are responsible for them, sir.

S: The debts you have accumulated in the incalculably long period of *saṃsāra* are with you. If you don't apply the Buddha's teachings and practice them, you will accumulate the same debts again and again, billions of times in every split second. Are you able to count these debts?

D: No, sir, they are incalculable.

S: Therefore, you should apply this practice the Buddha taught. If you don't accept what arises and disintegrates of its own accord, then your accumulated debts will diminish and no new debts will accumulate. If you realize this arising and vanishing for yourselves, then you don't make new debts and you get rid of the old ones. Thus you attain to real wisdom.

This technique of being aware of in-breath and out-breath can be practiced anywhere. You can practice it while you are alone or in company, while you are sitting, walking, standing, or lying down. Wherever you are, you can practice it. Now, do you have to spend money in order to practice Ānāpāna?

D: No, sir.

S: Do you have to take time off work to practice?

D: No, sir.

S: In that case, what is so difficult about it? Will this practice make you feel tired?

D: No, sir.

S: If you make great profits with your business and people ask you, "How much gold, how much silver have you got?", will you tell them?

D: No, sir.

S: And why not?

D: One shouldn't tell others such things, sir.

S: Now, which jewel is more precious, gold and silver, or the Dhamma?

D: The Dhamma is more precious, sir.

S: Then don't talk to others about your achievements. What is the time now?

D: Seven P.M., sir.

S: How much time have you got left until sunrise?

D: About ten hours, sir.

S: Do you think that you can practice meditation for that long without a break? Work hard to rid yourselves of your debts. The efforts of the past and meritorious deeds performed in the past are giving their good results.

Discourse Three

Keep Your Mind on the Spot

Webu Sayadaw: You have undertaken to keep *sīla*. Having taken up the training in *sīla*, practice it to the utmost. Only if you really practice morality will the aspirations you treasure in your heart be fulfilled completely.

Once you are established in moral conduct, the skilful actions you undertake will result in the fulfilment of your noble aspirations. You believe in the benefits accruing to you from giving charity, and you respect the receiver of your gift. So, straighten your mind and give to the Dhamma which has no peer. Prepare your donations yourselves and prepare them well, without employing others for the purpose.

Giving your gift, you ought to aspire to awakening by saying: "I desire to attain Nibbāna" (*idaṃ me puññaṃ nibbānassa paccayo hotu*). The noble ones who attained Nibbāna according to their aspirations are so numerous that they cannot be counted.

The reality one realizes and knows for oneself after penetrating the Four Noble Truths is called *bodhi*. There are different types of *bodhi*: *sammā-sambodhi* (the supreme self-awakening of a teaching Buddha), *pacceka-bodhi* (the self-awakening of a non-teaching Buddha), and *sāvaka-bodhi* (the awakening of a disciple of a teaching Buddha). The *sāvaka-bodhi* is divided into three levels: *agga-sāvaka-bodhi* (attained by the two chief-disciples), *mahā-sāvaka-bodhi* (attained by the eighty leading disciples) and *pakati-sāvaka-bodhi* (attained by all other Arahats). All of us have to aspire to Nibbāna, the highest blessing. Why can you bring your aspirations to Nibbāna to fulfilment now? Because the time is right, your form of existence[16] is right, and because of the fact that all virtuous people who put forth effort can fulfil their aspirations.

The right time is the time when a Buddha arises and the time during which his teachings are available. All those who are born in the human plane or in a celestial plane are said to have the right birth. Now you have to fulfil your aspirations through your own effort.

See to it that you bring your work to a conclusion in the way so many before you have done. Once they reached their goal they were truly happy not only for a short time, or for one lifetime, but for all the remaining lives.[17]

Now that you do have this aspiration for Nibbāna, do not think that you can't attain to such happiness or that you can't fulfil such a high aspiration. Establish energy and effort sufficiently strong for you to reach the goal. If you do so, you will beyond all doubt realize your aspiration at the right time.

What will you know once you have done the work that has to be done? At the time of the Buddha, people, *devas*, and *brahmās* went to him to pay their respects. But no human being, *deva*, or *brahmā* was satisfied just by being in the presence of the Buddha and by paying homage to him. So, the Buddha out of compassion wanted to teach them what he had discovered and understood for himself. This communicating of his knowledge we call preaching. When the Buddha preached, in one split second many people, *devas*, and *brahmās* attained what they had been aspiring to.

Knowing that this is the right time and the right form of existence, we should establish awareness as the wise people did before us and thus we can experience the fulfilment of our aspirations.

What are the teachings of the Buddha? The monks and the wise people have passed on the teachings of the Buddha to you out of great compassion. Every time you were instructed, you understood some of it, according to your capability to understand. You know that the teachings are enshrined in the Tipiṭaka, the Three Baskets. You know: "This is from the Sutta-piṭaka. This is from the Vinaya-piṭaka. This is from the Abhidhamma-piṭaka." All of you know a lot about the teachings.

The holy scriptures are very extensive. Even though the wise read, study, and teach these scriptures without interruption, they are too extensive for one person to study and understand them completely. It is impossible for one person to master the whole of the scriptures because these contain all the teachings of the Buddha. They are complete, wanting in nothing. They represent what the Buddha has penetrated and understood for himself. The teachings contained in the Tipiṭaka are the only way of escape from suffering, and the monks, having understood this for themselves, out of compassion point this out to you again and again. But can the wise people expound all of the sacred scriptures to you, so that not a single aspect is left out?

Disciple: No, sir, this is impossible.

Sayadaw: How long would it take to expound all the teachings of the noble ones? How many days would you have to sit and talk in order to cover all the teachings of the noble ones that are remembered?

The purpose of all these teachings is to show the path to the end of suffering. You know quite enough of the teachings of the Buddha. In all these manifold aspects of the teachings you have to take up one and study it with perseverance. If you focus your mind on one single object, as the wise of old did, does it not stay with that object?

D: It does, sir.

S: So, select one instruction for meditation out of the many different ones the Buddha gave, and work with it, being aware always. Work with as much effort and determination as the disciples of the Buddha did in the past. If you focus your mind on one object, it will give up its habit of wandering off to objects it desires. When you are thus capable of keeping your mind on one single object, can there still be greed which is the cause of unhappiness?

D: When the mind is stable, there is no greed, sir.

S: Is there aversion?

D: No, sir.

S: Can there be delusion?

D: No, sir.

S: If there is no liking, disliking, and delusion, can there be fear, worry, and agitation?

D: No, sir.

S: If there is no fear, worry, and agitation, will you be happy or unhappy?

D: There will be happiness, sir.

S: If you choose an object of meditation given by the Buddha and practice with strong effort, will the *viriya-iddhipāda* factor[18] hesitate to arise in you?

D: It will not fail to come, sir.

S: As soon as you establish yourselves in effort, the *viriya-iddhipāda* factor will arise. But we are good at talking about the teachings. Let us instead put forth effort right away. The *viriya-iddhipāda* factor will arise immediately. This is called *akāliko*, the immediate result that arises here and now. It doesn't arise because we think or know about it, but only because of practice. So then, focus your entire attention at the spot below the nose above the upper lip. Feel your in-breath and your out-breath, and feel how it touches at the spot below the nose and above the upper lip.

I think you had your mind's attention focused on the spot even before I finished giving the instructions?

D: I don't think all were able to do that, sir.

S: Well, all understood what I said.

D: Some don't know yet how they have to practice, sir.

S: Oh my dear … you all have learned so much in the past. The monks taught you with great compassion time and time again, and you have grasped their instructions intelligently. When I told you to concentrate on the spot with strong determination and not to let your mind wander, you said it did stay with the breath, didn't you?

D: Those who had focused their mind on the spot answered, "It does stay, sir," but there are young people in the audience who have never heard the Dhamma before.

S: Did I say anything you haven't heard before? All of you are great lay disciples and have come so many times. All of you are capable of preaching the Dhamma yourselves.

D: Not all are, sir. Some don't know anything yet.

S: Can you others accept what he just told me?

D: Sir, I'm not talking about those people over there, I'm talking about some people not known to me.

S: In what I tell you there is nothing I have found out myself. I am only repeating to you what the Buddha preached. What the Buddha taught is without exception perfect, complete. What I preach is not complete. What the Buddha preached includes everything. His teachings are wanting in nothing, but what I am able to convey may be lacking in many aspects. Would I be able to give you all the teachings in their completeness?

D: No, sir, you can't tell us everything.

S: Well, all of you understand what the Suttas are, what the Vinaya is, and what the Abhidhamma is. Because your teachers have instructed you out of great compassion, you also understand the short and the more extensive explanation of *samatha*[19] and *vipassanā*. But whether you know all this or not, all of you breathe, big and small, men and women. One may know all about the Pāÿi scriptures, but nothing about his own breath. Don't all of you breathe in and out?

D: We do breathe, sir.

S: When do you start breathing in and out?

D: When we are born, sir.

S: Do you breathe when you sit?

D: Yes, sir.

S: Do you breathe in and out when you stand upright?

D: Yes, sir.

S: When you are walking?

D: We breathe in and out then too, sir.

S: Do you breathe when you are eating, drinking, and working to make a living?

D: Yes, sir.

S: Do you breathe when you go to sleep?

D: Yes, sir.

S: Are there times when you are so busy that you have to say, "Sorry, I have no time to breathe now, I'm too busy"?

D: There isn't anybody who can live without breathing, sir.

S: In that case all of you can afford to breathe in and out. If you pay close attention, can you feel where the breath touches when you breathe? Can you feel where the air touches when it comes out of the nostrils?

D: I can feel where it touches, sir.

S: And when the the air enters, can't you feel at which point this feeble stream of air touches?

D: I can, sir.

S: Now, try to find out for yourselves at which spot the air touches gently when it goes in and when it comes out. Where does it touch?

D: It touches at a small spot at the entrance of the nostrils when it enters, sir.

S: Does the air also touch there when it comes out?

D: Yes, sir, it touches at the same spot when it comes out.

S: Wise people of the past have practiced this awareness of the breath as the Buddha instructed them, and because they passed on the teachings, you too have understood now.

If you were to put your finger on the small spot under the nose, could you then feel that spot?

D: Yes, sir, I can feel it.

S: You can actually feel it when you touch it. Do you still have to talk about it?

D: No, sir, we can feel it even without talking about it.

S: As you can feel the spot when you touch it with your finger, you can also feel it when the breath touches there when it enters and leaves the nostrils. If you can feel it for yourselves, do you still have to talk about it?

D: No, sir, we don't have to.

S: If you put your finger on the spot, do you feel the touch sensation with interruptions or continuously?

D: It is a continuous touch, sir.

S: Is the stream of air entering or leaving ever interrupted?

D: No, sir.

S: As the air streams in and out we know its continuous flow and the continuous touch resulting from it. Don't follow the air to that side.

D: What do you mean by that, sir?

S: Don't let go of the sensation produced by the breath touching the skin. Remain with the awareness of touch. Don't follow the stream of air inside or outside. And why? If you do that, you won't be able to feel the touch sensation. So, let's stay with the awareness of the spot without a break.

D: Do we have to be aware of the touch of air in both nostrils or just in one?

S: Feel only one. If you try to feel two places your attention will be split. Put your undivided attention on one spot. Does your mind stay at the spot?

D: Most of the time it does, sir.

S: But not all the time?

D: Most of the time it stays, but at times the sound of coughing interrupts the continuity.

S: Is it your own coughing or is it someone else's?

D: It's someone else coughing, sir.

S: Does this disturb you because you put in too little effort or too much effort? Is the person who coughs to be blamed?

D: Well, sir, to be honest, I get a little bit angry.

S: Let's have a look at this. You have come to the Buddha to escape from suffering. Having received his teachings you begin to practice. Then someone coughs and you are upset. But of course, if you meditate, as you are doing now, people will consider you to be a good person and they will praise you. But tell me, if this good person becomes angry just before he dies, where will he be reborn?

D: He will fall into the four lower planes.

S: Yes, you should not allow this to happen. You shouldn't be impatient and short tempered. You are practicing in order to escape from suffering. Hearing this coughing you should be very happy. You should say "thank you." After all, the person who is coughing shows you that your effort isn't firm enough. If you want to escape from suffering, you have to do better than this. With this type of effort, you won't make it.

We should immediately put in more effort. If we work with more determination, will we still hear this coughing?

D: No, sir, not with good effort.

S: And if there are many people, all talking loudly, will we still hear them?

D: If our effort is not of the right type, we will, sir.

S: Should we become angry at them if we hear them?

D: Most times I do get angry, sir.

S: You should not allow this to happen. You should not be short tempered. You should think of the people who disturb you as being your friends: "They are concerned with my welfare, I should thank them. I don't want everyone to know that my effort is so weak. I will meditate and improve myself and if they begin to talk still louder, I have to put in even more effort." If we improve ourselves until we are equal in effort to the wise who have practiced before us, we will attain the goal to which we aspired.

If you don't hear any sounds at all, you become filled with pride, thinking that your effort is perfect. That is why we should be very happy if someone disturbs us. If we go to another place, there may be disturbances again. If we change from one place to another, we just lose time. But if we establish our mindfulness firmly, do we still have to change place or complain to others?

D: No, sir.

S: Is it not proper to say "thank you" to those who disturb us? They help us to learn how to overcome our wishes and desires, and we have to thank all who are our friends. If our effort becomes as strong as that of our teachers, we will not hear anything any more. We will be aware of one thing only: this small spot and the touch sensation. Once we have gained good awareness of this, we will apply our attention fully to this awareness.

If we attain to the happiness to which we aspire through this practice, are the contents of the Tipiṭaka, the ten *pāramīs*, the three fold training, the aggregates, the sense bases, and the relative and ultimate truths not all contained in this awareness?

D: Yes, sir, the awareness of this touch sensation contains everything that the Buddha taught.

S: You have been talking about the three Piṭaka, about the Four Noble Truths, about mind and matter, and other technical terms. But do you actually know how to distinguish between mind and matter? Is the small spot under your nose mind or matter?

D: It is matter, sir.

S: And what is the awareness of the spot?

D: That is mind, sir.

S: And if you are as clearly aware of this spot under your nose as when you touch it with your finger?

D: Then we are aware of mind and matter, sir.

S: Is it good or bad to be aware of mind and matter simultaneously?

D: It is good, sir.

S: Is this called understanding or ignorance?

D: It is understanding, sir.

S: And what if we don't have this awareness?

D: Then we live in ignorance, sir.

S: Which is more powerful, knowledge or ignorance?

D: Knowledge has more power, sir.

S: Yes, it is understanding that has power. The whole of the cycle of birth and death is full of ignorance, but now that you have received the teachings of the Buddha, be aware. Skilful people gain awareness because they are able to accept the teachings of the Buddha and direct their attention here only. As they gain awareness, knowledge comes to them. When you are aware in this way, what happens to ignorance?

D: It is cut off and disappears, sir.

S: Where can we find it, if we look out for it?

D: It is gone, sir.

S: Though ignorance has had so much power over you in the past of *saṃsāra*, when you receive the teachings of the Buddha and achieve understanding, you don't even know where your ignorance has gone. So, really, understanding has much more power than ignorance, and still you complain that ignorance has such a strong hold over your minds.

D: But, sir, we have been associated with ignorance for so long that we are reluctant to let go of it.

S: Still, if you apply the teachings of the Buddha, ignorance will disappear. Which of the two is more agreeable to you?

D: For us, sir, ignorance is more agreeable.

S: Would you like to sustain a state of understanding?

D: Yes, sir, but we can't let go of ignorance.

S: Does ignorance force its way into your mind?

D: We call it into our minds by force, sir.

S: All of you have had an education, and you know many things about the teachings of the Buddha, and you can talk about them, and you practice them. You meditate and keep up your awareness all the time. But tell me, what preparations do you have to make in order to meditate?

D: We have to take a cushion and a mat to lie down, sir.

S: If you have all these things, will your meditation be good as a matter of course?

D: We have to stay away from other people too, sir.

S: What happens if you are negligent?

D: We fall asleep, sir.

S: You are disciples of the Buddha. You know that ignorance is your enemy. And though you know that, you start meditating only after preparing a bed for yourself. After meditating for some time you will become bored, and sloth and torpor will creep in. What will you do then?

D: We will endure them.

S: And if sloth and sleepiness are very strong, will you still resist?

D: No, sir, we will say to them, "Now only you come!"

S: Yes, that's just like you! "Now only do you come! I have had the bed ready for a long time." That's what you are going to think, aren't you?

D: Yes, sir.

S: When will you wake up again after going to sleep?

D: We will get up when it is day and time for breakfast, sir.

S: If you go on speaking in this way, this will have the effect that the dangers of ignorance will never be overcome. You don't praise understanding and wisdom, but ignorance. If you work like this, will you ever obtain the happiness to which you have aspired?

D: No, sir.

S: Will you just pretend to work then?

D: If we just pretend, we won't get anywhere, sir.

S: So, if you can't achieve your goal, what will you do?

D: I think we will have to continue with this practice until we reach the goal, sir.

S: Good. Yes, you know the difference between understanding and ignorance. Knowing what to do to achieve understanding, focus your attention on the spot and then keep it there. If you live with this awareness, do you still have to fear and be worried about the moment of death?

D: No, sir.

S: Tell me, what happens if you die without this awareness?

D: I will be reborn in one of the four lower planes.

S: Do you want this to happen?

D: No, sir.

S: Do you really not want to go, or are you telling me a lie?

D: You are right, sir, I have fallen into telling lies. I am walking on the path that leads straight to the lower worlds. I am speaking only empty words when I say that I don't want to go to hell and am still staying on the broad highway leading downwards.

S: Very good. You have understood. If you know for yourself whether you have got some understanding or not, then you are on the right path. If you know when you don't understand, you have understood. But if you think you have understood though you haven't understood a thing, then there is not the slightest hope for you to acquire any understanding.

You see, he knows that he is lazy when he is lazy; he knows that he is useless when he is useless. If you can see yourself in the correct light, then you will achieve understanding, because you are able to correct yourselves.

"I don't want to go to the lower worlds. Well, with all the meditation I'm doing I'll be alright. After all it doesn't take that much." Do you still think in this way, assuming that you needn't work much anymore, when really you do?

D: No, sir, I don't take what is wrong to be right and what is right to be wrong.

S: If you firmly fix your attention on the spot and are aware of mind and matter, you practice understanding. If you have no awareness, you are living in ignorance. If you die with your mind steeped in ignorance, you will go down, even if you are observing the Uposatha precepts.[20] Tell me, where would you be reborn if you happened to be at a pagoda or under a Bodhi treewhen you die?

D: Wherever I am, if I can't concentrate my mind when I die, I will go down, sir.

S: What about monks? Suppose I think, "Ha, my stock of merit is quite great, much greater than the merit of those lay people," and then I wander about here and there with a smile on my face. If I were to die, where would I be reborn?

D: We don't dare to say anything about monks, sir.

S: You needn't say anything about monks, just take me as an example.

D: Sir, we would dare even less say anything about you.

S: I'm assuming that my mind wouldn't stay with any object and I had to die, what would happen, my disciple?

D: Sir, I don't think there is a time when you are not aware of this spot.

S: But if I were to die without this awareness?

D: If it were me, I would fall into the lower planes.

S: Whoever it is, if there is no awareness at the moment of death, the result will be rebirth in hell. Therefore, establish your mindfulness so that you never forget this small spot. If I were to wish to be reborn in hell after having reached complete understanding due to this awareness, would there be a possibility of my going to hell?

D: Such a wish couldn't come true, sir.

S: If we don't understand what should be understood, and then start praying for Nibbāna, will we get it?

D: No, sir. However long we pray for Nibbāna, we will go down.

S: Ignorance leads to the four lower worlds. But if you take up this training of awareness of in-breath and out-breath, you will gradually develop towards the attainment of Nibbāna to which you have aspired. So, place your attention at this small spot steadfastly so that it doesn't budge.

Isn't it possible for you to fix your mind on this small spot while you are sitting in front of me?

D: It is, sir.

S: Can it be done while standing and walking?

D: Yes, sir.

S: Can you practice while eating, drinking, or working?

D: It is possible, sir.

S: Can you practice *ānāpānasati* when you are alone?

D: Yes, sir.

S: Or when you are in a crowd?

D: Even then it is possible to keep up the awareness, sir.

S: Do you get tired if you keep your attention at the spot all the time?

D: No, sir, it is not tiresome.

S: Does it cost you anything?

D: No, sir, it doesn't cost anything.

S: Is your work interrupted or disturbed?

D: No, sir, it isn't.

S: Are you more efficient in your work if you let your mind wander here and there or if you keep your attention focused on the spot?

D: It takes the same amount of time, sir.

S: Who is more efficient, the one with a wandering mind or the one who keeps his mind under control?

D: The one who keeps his attention at the spot does his job, and at the same time he is working for the attainment of Nibbāna.

S: One may earn one hundred thousand, but the one who works and practices awareness at the same time earns twice as much. From now on you will earn two hundred thousand. But, tell me, when we make our mind firm and tranquil, will our reward be only this much?

D: No, sir, when the mind is clear it becomes stable, firm, and strong.

S: The housewives here are surely all experienced in cooking. You have to cook at times though you are very tired.

D: Yes, sir, at times we just stare into the fire and nod from fatigue. Then the rice is burned sometimes, sir.

S: Why does this happen?

D: Because our mind is not on the job, sir. Just yesterday I was thinking of some scene I had seen in a show and I burned the rice, sir. If my mind didn't wander, I would be able to do my work more quickly, and I wouldn't burn the food.

S: What happens if you eat rice that isn't properly cooked?

D: Some people get an upset stomach, sir.

S: If you cook in a haphazard manner, you are slow, you get tired easily, and the food isn't good. The fire burns down, and you have to kindle it anew. The water for the rice cools down, and you have to bring it to a boil again. Nothing is improved by not being attentive. When we improve our awareness, so many other things improve. I am only telling you what the Buddha taught, but of course I can't tell you all he taught. There are many more advantages resulting from this practice. The Buddha's teachings are complete and without a flaw. It is impossible to teach every aspect of the Dhamma. But if you keep your attention focused on the spot and are aware from moment to moment, then you will reach your goal. The Buddha did teach this, and the wise people of old did reach their goal by this practice, and yet there are many things the Buddha realized that are not contained in this. But you can reach your goal if you keep knowing in-breath and out-breath at the spot. You will become really happy.

I am talking only about this little spot. You know all the theories about meditation for tranquillity (*samatha*) and insight meditation (*vipassanā*) and how they come about. Yes, there is *samatha* and there is *vipassanā*, but the Buddha did say that you have to establish yourselves well in one practice:

> If you practice one, you accomplish one.
> If you practice one, you accomplish two.
> If you practice one, you accomplish three.

But these are mere words. We have to practice with effort equal to the effort of the wise people of old.

When we teach the Dhamma we have to distinguish between Sutta, Abhidhamma, and Vinaya according to the established order, but only after having practiced meditation to the same extent and with the same effort as the noble disciples of the Buddha will you really be able to explain the teachings.

Though I have explained the technique to you in the proper way, some of you may remain closed to it and without understanding. If I ask you about the house in which you are living, you will describe it to me accurately. If I were to think and ponder about your house, would I be able to visualize how it really is?

D: No, sir.

S: If I were to think and ponder all day and all night without even sleeping, would I find out about your house?

D: No, sir.

S: Tell me then, how can I find out for myself what your house looks like?

D: If you come to my house yourself, you will immediately know all about it even if no one says a word to you.

S: So, you too should proceed in such a way that you reach your goal. When you get there you will know, "Ah, this is it." Will you continue to put off practicing? No, of course not. You can attain the Dhamma here and now.

Understanding all this, practice, make effort. You told me just now that meditation doesn't tire you. You said that it didn't cost anything, it didn't disrupt your work, and that you were able to practice it while alone and while you are with your family. Can you still find excuses for not practicing, or are you going to continue living in the same way as you have been, without even trying to find excuses?

D: Most of the time we just carry on as usual, sir.

S: Those who take up this practice will receive the answers to their questions. So, keep your mind focused and your cooking will be done quickly; the rice is not going to be burned, and no wood is wasted. Your whole life will improve, and the time will simply fly.

There is right conduct, and there is understanding. Both are important. Right conduct is the fulfilment of your manifold duties and your giving of the four requisites for the support and furthering of the Buddha's teaching. The control over your mind gives you understanding.

There are these two elements of training, and you have to train yourselves in both simultaneously. Is it not possible to be aware of the breath while you are preparing and giving the four requisites to the community of monks?

D: It is possible, sir.

S: Under which of the two disciplines does sweeping fall?

D: Sweeping is part of right conduct.

S: Can't you keep your attention at the spot while you are sweeping?

D: We can, sir.

S: Under which of the two trainings does serving your parents fall, to whom you are deeply indebted for the love, compassion, and support they have given you?

D: That is right conduct, sir.

S: What do you accomplish if you keep your attention focused at the spot while you are serving and helping your parents?

D: We develop our understanding, sir.

S: So you can train yourselves both in right conduct and understanding at the same time. Sometimes you may say that you can't meditate, though you would like to, because you can't ignore your old father and mother. Does this happen to you?

D: Young people often think in this way and put off meditation, sir.

S: What about older people?

D: They often say they can't meditate because they have to look after their children, sir.

S: To fulfil our duties is part of moral conduct. If you don't fulfil your duties, your conduct is not perfect. At the same time that you fulfil your duties, admonishing your children, for example, you can train yourself in the awareness of the spot. Isn't this wonderful? Now you have the time to train yourselves in both moral conduct and understanding.

Venerate and respect your benefactors—your parents, your teachers, and the community of monks—without ever resting. From now on work without ever resting, with firm effort, as the wise of old did before you. Your aspirations will be realized as were the aspirations of the wise disciples of the Buddha.

Discourse Four
A Roof That Does Not Leak

Sayadaw: The contents of the Tipiṭaka taught by the Buddha are so vast that it is impossible to know all they contain. Only if you are intelligent will you be able to understand clearly what the monks have been teaching you out of great compassion. You have to pay attention only to this.

Disciple: Sir, we don't quite understand what you mean by: "You have to pay attention only to this."

S: Let me try to explain in this way. If you build a house, you put a roof on it, don't you?

D: Yes, sir, we cover our houses with roofs.

S: When you put the roof on you make sure that it is watertight, don't you? If you cover your house well and it rains a little, will the roof leak?

D: No, sir, it won't.

S: And if it rains very hard, will the roof leak?

D: No, sir.

S: And when the sun burns down, will it still give you good shelter?

D: It will, sir.

S: Why is this so? Because your roof is well built. Will you be able to know whether your roof is leaking or not after it rains?

D: Yes, sir, when it rains it is easy to find out.

S: You see, you think that the teachings of the Buddha are vast and varied, but really they are just one single way of escape from suffering. Only if you take up one object of meditation given by the Buddha and pursue it with steadfast effort to the end can you justly claim that your roof is not leaking any more. If your roof is not rain-proof yet, you have to be aware of this. There must be many houses in your neighbourhood and they all have roofs. What are the materials used for roofing?

D: There are corrugated iron roofs, there are tiled roofs, there are houses roofed with palm leaves or bamboo.

S: Yes, of course. Now, if a palm-leaf roof is well built, is it reliable?

D: Oh yes, sir, it won't leak.

S: If a tin roof is well assembled, is it rain proof?

D: Yes, sir, it is.

S: What about a well-made tile roof?

D: No rain will come through, sir.

S: What about bamboo roofs or roofs made out of planks?

D: If they are well done, they are watertight, sir.

S: So, if you take the roofing material you like best and build a good roof, will it give you shelter when it rains and when the sun shines?

D: If we build it well, it will not leak, sir.

S: We are building roofs because we don't want to get wet when it rains, and we want to avoid the scorching sun. The teachings of the Buddha are available now. Take up one of the techniques the Buddha taught, establish steadfast effort and practice. Only if you are steadfast does your practice resemble a roof, and greed, anger, and ignorance cannot leak through. Only if the roof is not leaking can we say that we are sheltered. If the roof is still leaking rain, is this because it is good or is not so good?

D: Because it is not so good, sir.

S: Is it leaking because the palm leaves are not a good roofing material?

D: No, sir, palm leaves are a good roofing material.

S: Or is it because corrugated iron, or tiles, or bamboo, or planks are not suitable as roofing materials?

D: No, sir, all these are quite okay.

S: Then why is the roof leaking?

D: Because it isn't well built, sir.

S: But, of course, the mistake is made now. Is it difficult to repair it?

D: If one is skilful, it is quite easy, sir.

S: Tell me then, if it leaks in a certain place, what do you have to do?

D: We have to patch up the leak, sir.

S: It is just the same in meditation. Now that you exert effort, there is no leak; you are safe. If greed, anger, and ignorance still drip in, in spite of your practicing the teachings of the Buddha, you have to be aware of the fact that your roof is not yet rain-proof. You have to know whether the roof you built for your own house is keeping the rain out or not.

D: Sir, we have all the roofing materials, but the roof is still leaking. We would like to know the technique of building a good roof.

S: Don't build a thin, shaky roof; build a thick, strong roof.

D: How are we to build a strong roof, sir? While we are sitting here like this, we still have to endure being drenched by the rain.

S: The wise people of old practiced the teachings without allowing their efforts to diminish in any of the four postures,[21] and they kept up such a perfect continuity of awareness that there never was any gap. You too have to practice in this way. The disciples of the Buddha established awareness of the spot and then did not allow their minds to shift to another object. Now, can the rains of greed, anger, and ignorance still affect those who are steadfast?

D: No, sir, they can't.

S: If you establish the same quality of awareness whether sitting, standing, or walking, will the rain still be able to penetrate your protecting roof?

D: Sir, please teach us the technique which will give us shelter.

S: Tell me, all of you are breathing, aren't you?

D: Oh yes, sir, all are breathing.

S: When do you first start breathing?

D: Why, when we are born of course, sir.

S: Are you breathing when you are sitting?

D: Yes, sir.

S: Are you breathing while you are standing, walking, and working?

D: Of course, sir.

S: When you are very busy and have a lot to do, do you stop breathing, saying, "Sorry, no time to breathe now, too much work!"

D: No, sir, we don't.

S: Are you breathing while asleep?

D: Yes, sir, we are.

S: Then, do you still have to search for this breath?

D: No, sir, it's there all the time.

S: There is no one, big or small, who doesn't know how to breathe. Now, where does this breath touch when you breathe out?

D: Somewhere below the nose or above the upper lip, sir.

S: And when you breathe in?

D: At the same spot, sir.

S: If you pay attention to this small spot and the touch of air as you breathe in and out, can't you be aware of it?

D: It is possible, sir.

S: When you are thus aware, is there still wanting, aversion, ignorance, worry, and anxiety?

D: No, sir.

S: You see, you can come out of suffering immediately. If you follow the teachings of the Buddha, you instantly become happy. If you practice and revere the Dhamma, you remove the suffering of the present moment and also the suffering of the future. If you have confidence in the monks and teachers, this confidence will result in the removal of present and future suffering.

The only way out of suffering is to follow the teachings of the Buddha, and at this moment you are revering the teachings by establishing awareness. Do you still have to go and ask others how the Dhamma, if practiced, brings immediate relief from suffering?

D: We have experienced it ourselves, so we don't have to go and ask others any more.

S: If you know for yourselves, is there still doubt and uncertainty?

D: No, sir, there isn't.

S: By keeping your attention at the spot for a short time only, you have understood this much. What will happen if you keep your mind focused for a long time?

D: Understanding will become deeper, sir.

S: If your time were up and you were to die while your attention is focused on the spot, would there be cause for worry?

D: There is no need to worry about one's destiny if one dies while the mind is under control.

S: This frees us from suffering in the round of rebirths, and having discovered this for ourselves, we need not ask others about it. If we establish strong and steadfast effort in accordance with our aspiration for awakening, is there still cause for doubt: "Shall I get it or shall I not?"

D: No, sir, we have gone beyond doubt.

S: So, then you have full confidence in what you are doing and due to your effort the *viriya-iddhipāda* factor arises. Suppose people come and say to you, "You haven't got the right thing yet; how could you ever succeed?" Will doubt arise in you?

D: No, sir.

S: You know that though you are certain that you will be able to reach the goal with your practice, other people might tell you that you will not.

D: Sir, knowing for oneself, one will not have doubts, whatever people may say.

S: What if not just a hundred people or a thousand people come to tell you that what you are doing is no good, but say the whole town?

D: Even if the whole town comes, no doubt will arise, sir.

S: Suppose the whole country came to contradict you?

D: Even so, sir, there will be no space for doubt to arise, because we realized this happiness for ourselves.

S: Yes, you know how much effort you have established. But don't think that your effort is perfect yet. You are only at the beginning. There is still much room for improvement. While you sit, walk, stand, and work it is always possible to be aware of the in-breath and the out-breath, isn't it?

D: Yes, sir.

S: If you focus your attention on the spot, are you unhappy?

D: No, sir.

S: Does it cost you anything?

D: No, sir.

S: The people, *devas* and *brahmās* who received the teachings after the Buddha's awakening practiced continuously, and therefore their respective aspirations for awakening were fulfilled.

What the Buddha taught is enshrined in the Tipiṭaka. If you keep your attention focused on the spot and on the in-breath and the out-breath, the whole of the Tipiṭaka is there.

D: We don't quite understand this, sir.

S: Oh dear. Why shouldn't you understand this? Of course, you understand.

D: But we would like to be certain that we understand this in detail, sir.

S: You have understood already. Have you checked whether all of the Buddha's teaching is contained in this awareness?

D: But, sir, our awareness is not deep enough to check this.

S: But you can talk about the Buddha's discourses, the monks' rules, and Abhidhamma philosophy.

D: When we discuss these, we just talk without really knowing.

S: Talking into the blue. Now, if you keep your attention at this spot, can you tell me whether the whole of the teaching is present there?

D: We don't know, sir.

S: Are you not telling me because you are tired?

D: No, sir, we aren't tired. We would like to answer.

S: If we want to make an end to suffering we have to observe the behaviour of mind and matter. Everyone says this. Matter is composed of eight basic elements. There are fifty-three mental concomitants.[22] All of you can tell me this off the top of your head.

You are intelligent. When others discuss the teachings you correct them and tell them where they went wrong and where they left something out. You refute them and criticize them. You are debating like this, aren't you?

We said just now that the thing that doesn't know is matter and the entity that knows is mind. These two entities must be evident to you. Under which of the two comes the spot below the nose; is it mind or matter?

D: I think that the spot is matter, sir. The *kāya-pasāda* (sensitive matter) through which we feel touch sensation is *rūpa*. But those who study Abhidhamma philosophy tell us that we are just concepts (*paññatti*) and that the spot too is but a concept, sir.... When we have debates with people who are proficient in the *Abhidhammattha-saṅgaha*[23] we become angry and agitated and get little merit.

S: If you can't keep your attention on the spot, you will of course get involved in discussions.

D: But, sir, if we don't answer, we have to admit defeat.

S: Tell me, what do you have to do when you are hungry?

D: We have to eat rice, sir.

S: What about monks, what do you have to give them to still their hunger?

D: We have to give them oblation rice,[24] sir.

S: Are the oblation rice they eat and the rice you eat two completely different things?

D: They aren't different, sir. In order to show respect to the monks we call their rice "oblation rice", but it is the same as we eat.

S: So, whether we call it "rice" or "oblation rice," it will satisfy our hunger.

D: Yes, sir, both fill the stomach.

S: Now what about the nose, the spot? You can call it by its conventional name, or you can talk about sensitive matter. It's just the same as with rice and oblation rice. Is it worth arguing about?

D: No, sir, there is no need for long discussions.

S: Having understood this, will you stop arguing, or will you carry on with your debates?

D: No, sir, we shall not debate, but those Abhidhamma students will.

S: In that case you just don't take part in the discussion of such issues. You have known all along that rice and oblation rice are the same, but we have to talk about it so that you understand. Now, what do we call the entity that is aware?

D: It is called mind, sir.

S: Only if you have gained such control over your mind that it doesn't jump from one object to another are you able to distinguish clearly between mind (*nāma*) and matter (*rūpa*).

D: Yes, sir, now we are able to distinguish between mind and matter.

S: Is this knowledge of mind and matter you have gained called understanding (*vijjā*) or ignorance (*avijjā*)?

D: It is understanding, sir.

S: Is there still ignorance present when you are able to distinguish clearly between mind and matter?

D: No, sir, ignorance has run away.

S: When you concentrate at the spot there is understanding, and ignorance has been banned. Now, if we continue to concentrate on the spot, will ignorance spring back up again?

D: No, sir, it won't.

S: Yes, you see, you have to establish understanding in this way. You have found it now; don't allow it to escape again. Can you again suddenly be overpowered by delusion if your understanding keeps growing moment by moment? Do good people still have to moan and complain, saying that it is difficult to get rid of ignorance once they have been given the teachings of the Buddha, which are the tools to overcome and defeat ignorance?

D: No, sir, they shouldn't complain. All they need to do is to put forth effort.

S: So, you realize that all the Buddha taught is contained in this meditation. If you put forth effort, establish yourselves in perfect effort, then you will reach full understanding. You told me that many types of material are suitable to build a good roof. Not only a tin roof or a palm leaf roof are safe; you can choose from many different materials. I think you have collected quite a variety of good roofing materials. Now you have to build a roof that really protects you against rain. Once you have built a good shelter, you won't get wet, and you won't have to suffer the heat of the sun anymore. If you build your shelter in the jungle, will it be good?

D: Yes, sir, it will.

S: If you build your roof in a city?

D: It will be safe, sir.

S: Does it make any difference whether you build your shelter in this country or in any other country?

D: Sir, it will give shelter here and there.

S: Are you happy if you're drenched by rain or if you have to live under the scorching sun?

D: No, sir, I would be unhappy.

S: In that case, put forth full effort so that you won't have to suffer sun and rain ever again.

Discourse Five
The Flight of an Arrow

Sayadaw: You have taken *sīla*. Having taken *sīla*, practice it. Only if you fulfil the perfection of morality completely can you be successful in attaining all the various aspirations for awakening without exception.

Now that you have understood that you have been born at an auspicious time and into a good existence, take up the practice of the teachings of the Buddha with all your strength and establish yourselves in them. The noble disciples of the Teacher practiced without slackening in their effort and were mindful in all the four postures of the body, without ever resting. They worked with steadfastness, and they all attained the goal they desired. You too should take up this practice with this strong will to reach your goal.

What is this practice without break or rest to be compared to? It is like the flight of an arrow. If we shoot an arrow with a bow, we take aim according to our desire. Now tell me, does the arrow at times slow down and then speed up again after we shoot it? Does it at times take rest and then again proceed toward the target?

Disciple: Sir, it flies fast and at a steady speed.

S: And when does it stop?

D: It stops only when it hits the target, sir.

S: Yes, only when it hits its aim, its target, does it stop. In just the same way did the direct disciples of the Buddha strive to attain the goal they had taken as their target. Moving at a steady pace without a break, without interruption, they finally attained that type of awakening (*bodhi*) they desired in their hearts.

Of course, there are various types of awakening. All of them can be attained if you work without resting. If you work for *sammā-sam-bodhi* (Buddhahood), you have to work continuously. If you work for *pacceka-bodhi* (Non-teaching Buddhahood), you have to keep up the continuity of practice. If you aim for *sāvaka-bodhi* (Arahatship), you have to practice steadily, just as an arrow flies steadily. If you practice with steadfastness you will be able to attain your goal.

Though you practice without interruption, you will not get tired or exhausted. As you take up the teachings of the Buddha, incomparable happiness will come to you.

Some people think that the Buddha taught many different things. You all remember some parts of the holy scriptures as the monks out of great compassion taught them to you. At times you may think, "The teachings of the Buddha are so vast and manifold. I can't follow and understand all this and therefore I can't attain my goal." Or some people say, "What is true for oneself one can only know oneself." Or others, "I can't work because I can't feel the breath yet." Now tell me what is your excuse?

D: Saying that we have to make a living to maintain our body, we postpone meditation from the morning to the evening and from the evening to the morning. In this way we keep delaying the work of putting forth effort.

S: And what else do people tend to say?

D: Some say they can't meditate because of old age and some are afraid that it will make them ill.

S: What do those say who are still young?

D: That they can't meditate because they have to study. While they are young and healthy they want to enjoy themselves.

S: And if you are unwell and ill?

D: Then, sir, we worry. We call the doctor and think about medicine, but we still don't practice.

S: And when you have recovered?

D: We somehow manage to postpone meditation day by day and let time pass.

S: But you do actually want to attain happiness, don't you?

D: Yes, sir.

S: So, if you really want it, why then postpone striving for it?

D: I don't want it really, sir.

S: Does this apply to you only or to all of you here?

D: There must be some in this audience who really aspire to attain happiness and others like me who are not so serious about it.

S: If you put forth effort as you are doing now, you will of course get it. But thoughts and doubts may come up in your minds, "Will I have to suffer? Will this practice be trying?" You have already acquired some knowledge of the Buddha's teachings according to your individual capabilities. Thinking about these, however, will slow down your progress. So listen well to the teachings now and practice. If you practice, you will arrive at your goal, and the reality of it may or may not correspond with your thoughts about it.

Only when you know for yourselves will you also know that your thoughts and speculations about the goal were not correct. All of you know from Dhamma lectures[25] that if you follow the teachings of the Buddha, you will get great happiness in the present and in the future. In fact, you are all preachers of the Dhamma yourselves. Don't you think that thinking and speculating will slow your progress down? If you think and analyze, will every thought be correct?

D: No, sir.

S: If you establish your goal as I told you and keep thinking about wanting to attain it, will this help?

D: No, sir.

S: So, will you continue to think and ponder?

D: If we analyze and think all the time we shall go the wrong way, sir.

S: Once we start thinking there will be very many thoughts. Will much of what we think be of use to us?

D: It is difficult to think useful thoughts. Thoughts often become quite useless and misleading.

S: The community of noble monks has expounded the teachings which are real and true to you and still your thoughts are apt to mislead you. How is this possible?

But tell me, where are you from?… You are from Kemmendine. Your house must have a garden and a fence around it.

D: Yes, sir, this is correct.

S: On which side of the compound is the gate?

D: I have one gate opening to the south and one opening to the north, sir.

S: How many stories does your house have?

D: It is a single storey house, sir.

S: On which side do you have your door?

D: There are two doors, sir, one in the west wall and one in the south wall.

S: So, now we know that you live in Kemmendine, that you have a fence around your garden with gates to the north and south. Your house is a one storey building and has two doors facing south and west respectively. You see, because you told me, I know everything about your place. Now my knowledge and your knowledge about your house are about the same, aren't they?

D: They cannot be, sir.

S: But why? You know your village, your garden, and your house; you told me that you live in Kemmendine; and you described your garden and your house to me as you know them. Therefore I know your village, your garden, and your house. I know the reality about it, as you do.

D: You don't know it in the same way I know it, sir.

S: My dear friend, why should what I know be different from what you know? Just ask me where you live and I shall reply that you live in Kemmendine. Furthermore, I know about your garden and house just as you do. What is there that you can tell me that I don't know already?

D: Even if I told you the house number and the street, you wouldn't be able to find the house, sir.

S: Tell me then what you know more about this matter than I do.

D: I can't tell you more about it, sir, but I know more because I have actually been there.

S: In that case I shall think about it and figure out where Kemmendine is.

D: You can't find out by thinking about it, sir.

S: I shall think a lot and for a long time. Some of it is bound to be right. I will think about a house in Kemmendine with two gates, two doors, one storey. Will some of my findings about your house be correct?

D: I don't think so, sir.

S: Is it that difficult then? Well, I'll think in many different ways; some of it will turn out right. I shall ponder over this problem for about one year. Will I find the answer then?

D: If you just think about it, sir, you won't find it. But if you come and look, you will really know for yourself.

S: Now, what if I were to think about it really deeply for about forty or fifty years? Or … better, if I don't just think but also talk about it. Will I come to know it then?

D: Even if you think and talk about it, sir, you will never get there.

S: Then please tell me where Kemmendine is.

D: From here you would have to walk towards the south-west.

S: So, if I walk in a southwesterly direction, will I get there?

D: Yes, sir, you will, but you will still not find my house.

S: Well I'll begin now. I'll think very deeply and at the same time I'll recite (your instructions and descriptions). In this way I'll come to know.

D: No, sir, I don't think so.

S: You tell me that you know all this about your house, but if I repeat what I know from you, then you tell me that I am talking into the blue. I cannot bear this.

D: Sir, you simply repeat what you heard, but you don't actually know.

S: So, all I say about this house is correct, but he claims that I still don't know it the way he does. I don't know whether this is true … But now if I were to think about it deeply and recite my thoughts, would there still be a difference in understanding? Or if I were to recite all you said day and night, would it still not be possible for me to really know?

D: Sir, you would still not know it in the same way you would if you went there yourself.

S: Before you told me about your house I didn't know anything about it, but now I know something.

D: Yes, sir, this is true, but if you came to see it you would know everything about it.

S: Tell me, if I were to walk according to your directions, would I arrive at your house?

D: Yes, sir.

S: And if I didn't know the house number?

D: You would wander aimlessly, sir.

S: And if you go there?

D: I head straight for my house, sir.

S: Will you worry about how to get there and whether you are on the right road?

D: If you come with me, sir, you can't get lost, because I have been there before.

S: The Buddha taught what he had realized for himself. Now, all of you are able to accept good advice. The Buddha's teachings are vast. There is the Suttanta, the Vinaya, and the Abhidhamma. You need not study all these. Choose one object of meditation, one technique that suits you, and then work with firm determination. Once you have established yourselves in this way and arrive at the goal, you will understand deeply and completely.

But even now, before I finish speaking, you do get some understanding. This immediate understanding is called *akāliko*,[26] immediate understanding.

Our teachers and parents, who instruct us out of great compassion and love, tell us: "Learn this and that …," and when we go to bed at night they call us and say: "Why didn't you pay respects to the Buddha before going to bed? Come, pay respects." If we don't follow their instructions, they may even have to beat us. They have to do this even though they don't wish to do it. Through their help these resistances in us are overcome. But, of course, we get immediate knowledge of the Buddha-Dhamma only if we are interested in it ourselves. When does it actually become *akāliko*, immediate?

D: Only when we really find the Dhamma, sir.

S: And when will we really find the Dhamma?

D: After having worked for it, sir.

S: At what particular time do we have to practice in order to be successful?

D: The hour of the day or night is of no importance. If we practice and then reach the goal we shall gain immediate knowledge, sir.

S: It is very easy. You have received the teachings of the Buddha. All you have to do is to make efforts in the same way that the disciples of the Buddha did. It is easy. This is not my own knowledge. I too have learned the teachings of the Buddha and I am passing them on to you. All of you are very intelligent and bright. What I am telling you, you know already. Why do you think the Buddha taught the Dhamma?

D: He taught people to be continuously aware of mind and matter.

S: He taught so that people who desire to attain the goal may be able to do so. He taught because he wished them to be able to travel on the path. But some of you may say that this is not a good time to practice. The mind is not settled with all this coming and going of people. "We shall meditate when the mind is tranquil," you may decide. And if the mind becomes tranquil after some time, what will happen?

D: When the mind is calm, we will go to sleep, sir.

S: Oh really, and this you call meditation?

D: Sir, we are only perfect in talking about meditation.

S: And then, when you have a bad conscience about not having practiced and decide to go to a meditation centre, what do you take along?

D: We take food with us, sir.

S: Tell me, after having taken the precepts, do you stuff yourselves?

D: Yes, sir. The ladies offer food, and we just eat. We start early, and then we continue eating right up until twelve noon.[27]

S: Do you eat more than on ordinary days?

D: Oh yes, sir, much more.

S: Tell me now, do you stop eating at noon?

D: Well, you see, sir, some say that even then it is all right to continue eating. Once one stops, then one can't start again after twelve noon, but if I started before noon I can continue eating even after midday. So I've heard.

S: What about you? Do you carry on eating?

D: I continue eating even while we are talking like this, sir.

S: And what do you do after you have finished eating?

D: Then my stomach is full, sir, so I lie down flat on my back.

S: And then?

D: Then I sleep, sir.

S: And when do you wake up again?

D: At about 3.00 or 4.00 P.M., sir.

S: Do you meditate then, being fully awake and alert?

D: No, sir, then I ask for some juice and lemonade.[27]

S: Do you drink a lot or just a little?

D: I drink to the full, sir.

S: Even if you drink a lot, some will be left over. Do you share that with others?

D: No, sir, I drink it all myself because I like to keep it for myself.

S: But do you feel good if you drink too much?

D: No, sir, not very good.

S: Tell me, do you meditate then?

D: Well, sir, as I don't feel very well I have to lie down.

S: And then what happens?

D: I sleep again, sir.

S: And when do you get up?

D: The following morning, sir, when the sun rises. I say to myself, "Well, look, the sun has risen," and I get up and have breakfast.

S: Now tell me, if you don't attain Nibbāna, do you think that it is because there is no such person as a fully awakened Buddha and that Nibbāna doesn't exist?

D: No, sir, it's because I eat too much.

S: Well, you do make some efforts, but this greed is still a little strong, I think. Tell me, when you start to meditate and someone whispers near your ear, do you hear it or not?

D: If the concentration is not so good, we prick up our ears and listen to what is being whispered, sir.

S: When you hear this whispering, do you accept it and respect the people who are whispering?

D: Sir, when the determination to meditate is strong, then I do get angry at the people who are whispering.

S: Meditators get angry?

D: If people come and whisper in the place where I'm meditating, of course I will get angry, sir.

S: Is it skilful to get angry and think, "Do they have to whisper here? Where is this chap from anyway? Who is he?" Will a meditator who reacts in this way attain his goal quicker? If he becomes angry and then dies, where will he be reborn?

D: He will be reborn in the lower worlds, sir.

S: Even if he is observing the eight Uposatha precepts?

D: If he becomes angry, he will go to the lower worlds even then, sir.

S: How should we approach the problem of being disturbed by whispers while we are meditating? We should reflect in the following way: "I have come here to meditate. My fellow meditators are whispering and I hear them. If the others find out that I pay attention to whispers, I will feel ashamed because all will know then that I don't make sufficient effort. I shall make more effort." We should be grateful to the people who show us through their whispering that our effort isn't sufficient. If your effort is good, your concentration will be good, and you won't hear anything. Being grateful, you should hope that these people continue talking, and you should continue to meditate. There is no need to go up to them and actually say, "Thank you." Simply continue to meditate, and as your awareness of the object of meditation becomes continuous, you don't hear disturbances any more. Would you hear people if they spoke quite loudly?

D: If they spoke loudly, I think I would hear them, sir.

S: Again we have to be grateful. "They are telling me to improve my efforts." Being grateful to those people, I steady my mind and focus on the spot again. To meditate means to be so closely aware of the object that it never escapes our attention.

D: Please, sir, explain to us how to be so closely aware of the object.

S: You just have to keep your attention fully collected, concentrated on the spot. All of you have been breathing ever since the moment you were born.

Can you feel where the air touches as you breathe in and out?

D: Sir, for me the touch sensation is most evident under the right nostril.

S: Not in two places?

D: No, sir, only in one place.

S: Yes, it touches at this small spot when you breathe in and when you breathe out. Tell me, does it enter with intervals or is it a continuous flow?

D: There are intervals, sir.

S: Is it the stream of air that is interrupted or the awareness of it? Is the touch of air continuous while you breathe in and out?

D: It is uninterrupted, sir.

S: Then you have to know this flow of air without interruption. Don't look elsewhere. Just know this touch of the breath. If you can't feel it, then try touching the spot of contact with your finger. When you know the sensation of touch, then take your finger away and stay with the awareness of touch-feeling at the spot. You have to become aware of the touch of air which is continuous as being continuous. If you are aware of this spot without a gap in the continuity of awareness, will you still hear whispers?

D: No, sir, I don't think so.

S: If the attention is firmly and steadfastly anchored at this spot, will you hear loud voices?

D: No, sir.

S: You know this spot below the nose above the upper lip so exclusively that you don't hear sounds any more. Is this spot matter (*rūpa*) or mind (*nāma*)?

D: It is matter, sir.

S: And the entity that knows it, that which is aware, what is it?

D: That is mind, sir.

S: So, if you are aware of the spot without interruption, you are continuously aware of mind and matter, are you not?

D: Yes, sir, this is true, sir.

S: If you are aware of mind and matter in this way, you know that there is no self, there is no man, there is no woman, there are no human beings or *devas* or *brahmās*? This is what the Buddha taught. If we are aware of mind and matter, do we still think in terms of human beings, *devas*, and *brahmās*?

D: No, sir, we don't.

S: Is it easy to be thus aware?

D: Yes, sir, it is easy.

S: This is knowing things as they are. Mind and matter arise without interruption. They arise and then disintegrate. How many times do they disintegrate in a flash of lightning?

D: I have heard that they disintegrate one hundred billion times in the wink of an eye, sir.

S: Tell me then, how can you count to one hundred billion in the wink of an eye?

D: I can't, sir.

S: Suppose you were given one hundred billion gold coins and would have to count them, how long would it take you?

D: I think it would take about a month, sir. Even if I were to count greedily day and night, it would take about that long.

S: The peerless Buddha penetrated all this with his own super-knowledge and then was able to teach it. But what can we know for ourselves? We can know mind and matter simultaneously. And what will we get from this awareness? We will be able to understand the characteristic of their behaviour. You needn't do anything special. Just practice as you are practicing now. Keep your attention focused on the spot and as you gain the ability to keep your attention with the awareness of breathing and the spot, mind and matter will talk to you.

D: Do we have to think of *anicca* (impermanence) when one in-breath comes to an end, sir?

S: It is good if you think of *anicca* as a breath comes to an end. If you know *anicca* in this way, will you be able to attain Nibbāna?

D: Not yet, sir.

S: So if you can't get Nibbāna yet, keep concentrating on the spot and you will come to know.

D: What do we have to know as being impermanent, sir?

S: You say that sugar is sweet, don't you? But if I have never before tasted sugar, how are you going to explain sweetness to me?

D: It is much better than even palm sugar, sir, but we can't explain it so that you will really know.

S: But you have tasted it, so why can't you tell me about it?

D: Well, sir, sugar looks like salt, but ants don't go for salt while they do like sugar. But this won't help you very much, sir. You have to taste it, sir.

S: So salt and sugar look similar. Now, if I eat some salt, calling it sugar, will I taste sugar?

D: No, sir, salt will remain salty.

S: In that case I'll think that sugar is salty.

D: This is just the same as us not knowing how to recognize impermanence, sir.

S: When we talk about the outer appearance of sugar, there are many possibilities of mistaking something else for sugar. Only if you explain the taste of sugar properly can I understand.

D: We would like to advise you to eat some sugar, sir.

S: Will you have to sit next to me while I'm eating it and say, "It is sweet, it is sweet ..."?

D: If I recited this, it would just bother you, and it isn't necessary to do this for sugar to be sweet. As soon as you put sugar into your mouth, you will be able to taste its sweetness, sir.

S: But let's say there is a jungle bhikkhu who wants to taste sugar. Will the sugar think: "This is a jungle bhikkhu. I won't be fully sweet for him. I shall be only half as sweet for him as I am for people in towns"?

D: Sugar isn't partial, sir; it is as sweet for one as for the other.

S: It is just the same with the awareness of mind and matter. If you keep up this awareness you will taste the Dhamma immediately, just as you taste sweetness when you eat sugar. Is it possible that you still mistake salt for sugar? You go to the market so many times, and you can easily distinguish between salt and sugar. You are not going to buy salt for sugar. The peerless Buddha penetrated the truth and really knew it. He can distinguish between what is liberation and what is suffering, and therefore he gave this liberation to human beings, *devas*, and *brahmās* alike. He just asked them to "eat." Just eat, it's real. Will you remain here without eating,afraid that it could turn out not to be true liberation?

D: We haven't reached that point yet, sir. We are just listening to your words.

S: Eat as I told you. You will not go wrong. And why can't you go wrong? Because mind and matter are actually arising and disintegrating continuously.

Why should you concentrate on the spot, though you don't know liberation yet? If you don't eat something, will you ever know what it tastes like? You know a lot about the Dhamma. You know about *nāma* and *rūpa*; you know what the Suttas are and you know about the Vinaya and the Abhidhamma. You know this is *samatha*, this is *vipassanā*.

D: But, sir, all this is mixed up in our head like a giant hodgepodge.

S: Let it be a mix up. Pay attention to this spot only, as I taught you. Later this mix up will be disentangled, everything will fall into place. If we go east we will get to a place in the east; if we go west we will arrive at a place in the west. The spot is like a vehicle. If you want to go to Mandalay, you have to board a train to Mandalay and stay on it. The spot is like the train; don't leave it. Keep your attention focused on it very closely. This is all I have to say. There is nothing to be said apart from this.

Do you know the eight constituents of the Noble Eightfold Path? How do you think they apply to this practice of concentrating on the spot?

D: If one concentrates on the spot with right concentration then one attains the knowledge of right view, sir.

S: Are the other elements of the Noble Eightfold Path pertinent to this practice?

D: Sir, the eight constituents of the Noble Eightfold Path are:[28] (1) right view, (2) right thought, (3) right speech, (4) right action, (5) right livelihood, (6) right effort, (7) right mindfulness, (8) right concentration. When our mind is fixed on the spot, we don't think unskilful thoughts in any way. Therefore right thought is there, sir. As we are not talking at all, we don't speak lies and therefore there is right speech. As awareness of breathing is a good action, right action is included in this practice. There is right livelihood too, as we are not trying to make a living by deceiving others, sir. We are putting our entire effort into keeping our attention on the spot, so there is right effort. Because we focus our attention on the breath without letting go, we have right mindfulness, and as the attention remains at the spot without wandering here and there, we have attained right concentration.

S: So, do you think this is like a boat or a train?

D: Yes, sir, it is like a boat, a train, or a cart or car that takes a person to his goal.

S: Do not leave this vehicle, do you understand? Keep your attention firmly focused here, on the spot, and never leave this spot. In this way you will reach your goal.

Sometimes you may become impatient travelling on the train to Mandalay and think, "I want to go to Mandalay, but is this train really going there or is it going to Rangoon?" If this happens, will you get off? Don't! Continue on your journey and you will see that you will eventually arrive in Mandalay.

If you get fed up and bored, don't leave the train. When you are enjoying yourselves, don't get down. When you are ill, stay on the train, and stay also when you are strong and healthy. When you have plenty of company, stay. When you are all alone, don't leave. When people say unpleasant things to you, persist, and when they speak to you respectfully, don't get off your train. What would you do if people were to hit you because they don't like you?

D: Sir, I think I would run away.

S: Just keep your attention on the spot. Even if robbers hit you, they can't strike down this awareness.

D: True, sir, but I think this awareness would go if they struck me.

S: Not necessarily. Our Bodhisatta, in one of his lives, became the king of monkeys.[29] One day he found a brahman who had fallen down a precipice in the jungle and was helpless and certainly going to die down there. This brahman was lamenting his fate and crying, "Oh poor me, I have fallen into a chasm a hundred yards deep. I shall certainly die down here. Oh poor me, oh, oh, oh… My relatives and friends, my wife and children, don't know about my misfortune. Nobody is here to help me. Oh, oh …," and he cried.

Now, noble beings are always concerned with the welfare of all beings, without exception. And as the Bodhisatta was such a noble being, he who was then the monkey king felt pity for the brahman in the same way he would have felt pity for his own children. And so he climbed down the precipice and went up to the brahman. "Do not fear, do not despair, I won't let you die. I shall take you back to the place you want to go," he said to the brahman to reassure him and to cheer him up. And he meant it too. But he wasn't ready yet to put him on his shoulders and carry him up the rocks, because he was afraid that he might fall and that the brahman might be hurt. He took a big rock of about the same weight as the brahman, put it on one shoulder and tried to carry it up the precipice, jumping from rock to rock. Only after having passed this test did he carefully take the brahman on his shoulders and climbed back up jumping from one boulder to the next.

After this great effort, the monkey king was exhausted. He was happy while performing this good action, but he was still happier when he had accomplished it and had saved a life. He was confident that the brahman he had saved from certain death was trustworthy, and said, "After carrying you up, I am a little tired. Please keep watch for a while so that I can rest." Then he placed his head in the brahman's lap thinking himself well protected from all the dangers of the jungle. But while the king of the monkeys slept, the brahman thought, "I shall go back home soon, but I have nothing to give to my wife and children. I shall kill this big monkey and give his flesh to them as a gift." He took the rock the Bodhisatta had carried up for the test-run and dealt the Bodhisatta's head a deadly blow. He didn't do this hesitatingly, feeling sorry for his saviour, but he hit him hard, so as to kill him with the first blow.

When the Bodhisatta felt the pain of the blow, he quickly climbed the next tree, and he asked himself who or what had attacked him. He then saw that there was no enemy around, but that the brahman himself had tried to kill him. He thought to himself: "Yes, there are people like this in the world too." As the Bodhisatta was thinking this, the brahman started lamenting again, exclaiming that he was lost in this big jungle and that he would perish after all. But the monkey king said to him, speaking from the tree, "Don't worry; don't be afraid. I have promised to take you back to your home and I shall not break this promise. I shall take you home. I can't carry you on my shoulder any more, but as you opened my skull, there is blood dripping to the ground continuously. Just follow the track of blood I shall make for you from up in the trees."

This is how the Bodhisatta acted. He took all this on himself because his goal was Omniscience, Buddhahood. He worked on all the ten *pāramīs*.

Did the Bodhisatta turn away from accomplishing the good deed he had undertaken to complete because he was afraid that the man who had attempted to take his life might again try to kill him? Did he abandon him in the jungle?

D: No, sir, the Bodhisatta led the brahman home with great loving kindness, in order to perfect his *pāramīs*.

S: You see, if one aspires to omniscient Buddhahood, one has to fulfil the perfections, the ten *pāramīs* in this way, without ever taking a break, without ever resting. Otherwise one can't attain Buddhahood. Do you understand? One never rests, one never becomes lax, but works on the ten perfections all the time.

You told me only a moment ago that you couldn't keep up your awareness if robbers attacked you and tried to kill you?

D: I couldn't keep it up as yet, sir.

S: But you are aspiring to awakening, aren't you?

D: Yes, sir, I am.

S: If you want it you can achieve it. If you keep your attention focused as I taught you, you will get much out of it, even if people should hit you, pound you, and destroy you. Have you heard the story of Tissa Thera?[30]

D: No, sir, I haven't.

S: Tissa Thera received the teachings of the Buddha and appreciating their value he thought: "Now I can't continue living in this grand style." So he gave all his possessions to his younger brother. He became a monk and went to live and meditate in the jungle with his begging bowl and his set of three robes.

Now his brother's wife thought: "It is very enjoyable to possess all the riches of my husband's older brother. If he remains a monk we shall have these riches for the rest of our life. But maybe he will not attain awakening, and then he may possibly return to lay life. So, I had best have him killed." And she gave money to some robbers and said to them, "Go and kill Tissa Thera. I shall give you more money after you have completed the job."

So, the robbers went to the forest where Tissa Thera lived and grabbed him. He said, "I don't possess anything, but if you want to take my bowl and my robes, please do so."

"We only want to kill you," the robbers replied. "Your brother's wife gave us money to kill you, and she will give us more still after we have completed the job. That is why we have to kill you."

Tissa Thera thought, "I am not emancipated from suffering yet," and he felt ashamed of himself. He said to the robbers, "Yes, yes, you have to kill me, but please give me until dawn and then only make an end to my life."

The bandits replied, "Everyone is afraid of death, and if this monk escapes, we shall not get our money."

"You don't trust me?" Tissa Thera asked. "Well, I shall make you trust me." And he took a rock and smashed both his legs. Then he said, "Now I can't run away any more, so please don't kill me until dawn."

Though the robbers were very rough people, due to the loving kindness of Tissa Thera they felt compassion and decided to let him live until daybreak.

Tissa Thera admonished himself: "Venerable Tissa, there is not much time left, dawn is close. Put forth effort!" He put forth strong effort in the practice of the Buddha's teachings, and as he worked with a steady mind, dawn arrived. As the sun rose, he fulfilled his aspiration and attained happiness. "I have attained release from the cycle of birth and death!" he rejoiced. He then woke the robbers and said, "The day has dawned, rise and come!" And he was full of joy. Now, was Tissa Thera a real disciple of the Buddha, an Arahat?

D: Yes, sir, he was.

S: Who has faster development do you think, someone who meditates with both legs broken, or someone who meditates as you do?

D: Sir, I would prefer to meditate without first breaking my legs.

S: Tissa Thera got it before dawn even with both his legs broken. Will you get it before the day breaks?

D: I don't think that I could get it, sir. It will take me longer than that. We take it easy, sir. If one doesn't have to break one's legs, effort is less, and progress therefore slower.

S: In that case, you are not so eager to attain your goal quickly?

D: Sir, we like to go slowly, slowly.

S: Well, then maybe you should break your legs and then meditate.

D: I don't have the courage to do that, sir. I say that I aspire to Nibbāna, but in my mind I am still fearful. I don't have the strength to accept being killed after breaking my own legs.

S: In that case, work just the same, but without breaking your legs.

D: We shall work hard in the way you taught us, sir. We are emulating Visākha and Anāthapiṇḍika, sir.[31] It says in the scriptures that they are enjoying a good life in the *deva* planes now and we would like to have that same type of enjoyment also, sir.

S: They are enjoying a good life after having attained a lot. But you have not attained to the same stage yet, have you? Are you really doing as they did? Anāthapiṇḍika went to Rājagaha as a banker on business. Only when he reached there did he come to know that a Buddha had arisen in the world. He didn't go to Rājagaha to meditate or to pay respects to the Buddha. But when he was told about the Buddha, he went to him immediately, in the middle of the night. He had to leave the city walls to go to the place where the Buddha resided. When he stood before the Buddha, he attained what he had aspired for. If someone drops everything and hurries to the Buddha in the middle of the night, is the effort of that person great or small? Do you think he ever let go of the Buddha as the object of his mind while on the way to him?

D: No, sir, he didn't.

S: Now, tell me about yourselves.

D: We lose the awareness of the object while we walk, or while we think and so on, sir.

S: If you want to become like Anāthapiṇḍika, you have to strive as he strove.

D: Anāthapiṇḍika had to go through a cemetery[32] on his way to the Buddha, sir. That much we can do too, sir.

S: It is said that Anāthapiṇḍika began his meditation in the first watch of the night and attained stream-entry (*sotāpatti-magga-phala*)[33] when the day broke. But if you can't get it by daybreak, never mind. It is good enough if you can get it by the time the sun has risen and it is light. Tell me, will you work so that you can attain the goal by tomorrow?

D: Sir, we too shall go through a cemetery to come to your monastery and in this way we shall emulate Anāthapiṇḍika.

S: Did he allow the continuity of awareness to be interrupted?

D: He didn't, sir, but we are doing the same as he did only as far as the way is concerned.

S: If you really want to become like Anāthapiṇḍika, you have to work. If you work, you can fulfil your aspiration. If you don't work, you won't achieve anything. Is it not possible for you to concentrate on the spot where the air touches?

D: It is possible, sir.

S: To become like Anāthapiṇḍika you have to practice as I taught you. Will you tell me tomorrow that you attained your goal?

D: I shall tell you that I haven't attained it yet, sir.

S: Do you know how much Anāthapiṇḍika did after he had attained the first stage of awakening? He thought, "This is incomparable! My king, my people, my relatives, my sons and daughters, the city dwellers and country folk, all of them have not yet heard that a Buddha has arisen. I want them to experience the same bliss I have experienced. Now, how can I accomplish this? I have to invite the Buddha and make him stay for some time in my city, Sāvatthī, and all can go and meet him. The Buddha, out of great compassion, will teach them, and at the end of the teaching human beings and gods alike will attain the bliss I have attained."

Anāthapiṇḍika understood the ultimate truth, and he knew the reason he understood it. He invited the Buddha in order to help others to understand too. He had rest houses built every ten miles along the road from Rājagaha to his native city. In Sāvatthī he built the Jetavana monastery for the Buddha, and he arranged everything in such a way that there was a place for everyone. He provided everything, giving to all, from beggar to the king. Thanks to Anāthapiṇḍika's arrangements, the people who met the Buddha on his journey to Sāvatthī gained benefits also. During the the Buddha's journey, many people, *devas*, and *brahmās* attained what they had aspired to. How many do you think were those who benefited?

D: We don't know, sir.

S: How many human beings, how many celestial beings attained Nibbāna then?

D: A great many, sir.

S: How many beings fulfilled their aspiration in the wink of an eye? It was 180 millions of *brahmās* and one *asaṅkheyyā*[4] of *devas*. How many beings attained awakening as time went by?

D: They must be innumerable, sir.

S: Anāthapiṇḍika continued to support the teaching of the Buddha and due to his effort many attained the Deathless. Understanding this, you have to make a lot of effort to attain your goal by tomorrow. Will you do this?

D: Do not think too highly of me, sir. I don't think I am able to get it by tomorrow.

S: You are hungry and your wife offers you food, but still you don't eat?

D: When it comes to food, I will even force my way to the table, sir.

S: Do you eat even though you don't want to eat or because you want to eat?

D: Because I want to eat, sir.

S: For how long is your hunger appeased if you eat once?

D: For about half a day, sir.

S: For how long will your hunger be stilled if you eat the way Anāthapiṇḍika ate?

D: For the remainder of the cycle of birth and death, sir.

S: Tell me, what is the best for you? The food your wife offers you and that keeps you satisfied for half a day, or what the Buddha offers you that keeps you satisfied for the remainder of the cycle of birth and death?

D: I have to answer that what the Buddha offers is best for me, sir.

S: You eat what your wife offers you. What then do you do with the food the Buddha offers?

D: I'm hesitant about that, sir. That's why I don't approve of myself, sir.

S: Good, good. Work hard. You put so much effort into doing all these other things because you don't view mind and matter properly. But you do feel respect for the Buddha. Having decided to meditate, meditate. As you meditate you may find that your limbs ache and become stiff. Now, don't think: "Why do I get this pain? Is it dangerous?" But make a resolve: "Let it be dangerous! If I have to die, so be it. I have died in the past too." How many times have you died, do you think?

D: Innumerable times, sir.

S: Tell me, have you ever died while you were meditating?

D: No, sir, I have died while being unskilful only. That is why I am still so agitated.

S: So, if we have to die, how should we look at it? "I have never died so far while meditating. I shall not wait until dawn. Let me even die right now, so that I can get the experience of dying while meditating." You should think in this way. If you die while meditating, will you become miserable?

D: No, sir.

S: If you live a life of laziness and sloth, will you become happy?

D: No, sir. I shall continue going round in the cycle of birth and death, *saṃsāra*, sir.

S: "I have never, in the whole of *saṃsāra*, had stiff and aching limbs because of meditation. It is good if I experience these troubles now." Thus should you look at your pains. Even though your limbs ache, do not give up. Know that wise people of the past have walked on the same path. You have to work. If you only talk about putting forth effort, you will not attain anything. Only if you meditate can you come to understand. Now you are probably thinking: "We want to meditate, but this venerable monk is talking for a long time." So, focus your mind now as the Buddha taught you to, and meditate with firm effort and perseverance.

Discourse Six

Work Without Wavering!

Webu Sayadaw: You have taken the precepts. Now that you have undertaken the practice of the perfection of morality, fulfil it.

What you realize when you penetrate the Four Noble Truths is called *bodhi*. You are born at a good time and in a good form of existence. Now then, emulate the wise disciples of the Buddha and put forth effort as strong as theirs, so that you may attain the awakening to which you aspired. Those who received the teachings from the Buddha himself worked ceaselessly in all four postures[35] and thus attained enlightenment.

The human beings, *devas*, and *brahmās* who achieved their aspiration [to awakening] on just one occasion cannot be counted in hundreds, thousands, hundred of thousands, or millions. Sometimes in one split second, an incalculably large number of beings achieved their aspirations. From the time the Buddha attained full awakening, beings have been able to attain Nibbāna. But it is not only during the lifetime of the Buddha that beings can attain Nibbāna; Nibbāna can be attained as long as the teachings of the Buddha are available.

The attainment of Nibbāna is not blissful just for a brief moment. It will have lasting effects for the rest of the round of birth and death (*saṃsāra*). What the Buddha taught is the way out of suffering. You don't have to know a vast amount. If you practice one technique properly, with strong and steadfast effort, you will come to know for yourselves that you are people of great strength. You will not have to ask others about the teachings, and you will not even have to tell others that you are practicing.

Once you have established effort, you will not only know what good teachers told you, but you will clearly know for yourselves how the *viriya-iddhipāda* factor[36] arises in a split second.

You have the good quality of being able to follow the good advice of the Buddha as his disciples did in the past.

When I increase effort, then the *viriya-iddhipāda* factor will increase also. And then what will happen? I will think "With just this much effort, the *viriya-iddhipāda* factor has arisen to this extent. But my energy is not exhausted yet. There is still more. I shall increase my effort further." And the will to increase effort will arise. At this same instant, effort increases. As effort increases, the *viriya-iddhipāda* factor becomes stronger. When these factors have thus risen to a very high standard, then all your aspirations can be fulfilled.

Do not take rest. Do not take breaks or time off. Work continuously. If you develop continuously, you will become happier and happier. In this way the disciples of the Buddha became very happy, never getting enough of this happiness. Do you understand?

If a king rules over a country, does he say complacently, "This one country is enough for me"?

DISCIPLE: No, sir, he doesn't remain satisfied.

S: And if he rules a whole continent and has become emperor, is he satisfied then?

D: No, sir, he isn't.

S: If he isn't satisfied, what will he do?

D: He will try to acquire more and more territory, sir.

S: When a man is emperor over a continent, he wants the whole world. When he gets the whole world, he wants to become a universal monarch.[37] Once he is a universal monarch will he say, "This is enough" and be satisfied?

D: No, sir, he will not be satisfied.

S: All those who are perfect in their faith and have performed the highest form of generosity and demonstrated the greatest form of respect can't be satisfied. They will practice meditation and will gradually attain the stages of awakening (*samāpatti*). Once they are able to enter into the states of Nibbāna, only this happiness will count for them.

Nibbāna is the highest and noblest form of happiness there is. It is said that one can never experience enough of the highest and noblest form of happiness. And not only the direct disciples of the Buddha were able to achieve it. If you put forth continuous effort to the same extent that the wise of old did, you too will experience this highest happiness, even now. Then you will know, "I experienced a happiness that doesn't last only for a moment, or just for a lifetime, but for the remainder of the cycle of birth and death. And why did I attain this happiness? Because I was born into the right form of existence, because I was born at the right time, because I put forth strong effort."

At any time when human beings, *devas*, and *brahmās* accepted and practiced the teachings, they were successful. In this context, "At any time" means that whenever one undertakes this practice, one obtains understanding. The time span in which the teachings of the Buddha are available is very important and special: if you want to attain Nibbāna you can do so at any time; it is easy now.

Don't say, "This isn't my cup of tea. This isn't suitable for me. I won't get anything out of this." You have noble aspirations and you can fulfil them now. So if you say to yourselves, "I shall take up the practice right now," don't you think you can get real understanding? You can get it practicing in a group or by yourself. Seek for yourself. Take up one of the techniques the Buddha taught and practice it with one-pointedness and strong effort. Establish awareness of in-breath and out-breath and the spot where the air touches while you are breathing in and out.

When you are thus aware of the spot, can there still be worry, anxiety, and fear? Can there still be greed, aversion, and delusion?And, when you concentrate your mind in this way, you revere the teachings, don't you?

D: Yes, sir.

S: You will understand that the degree to which you come out of suffering depends on how much effort you put in and on how strongly the *viriya-iddhipāda* factor arises out of this effort.

D: We understand, sir.

S: There will be no more room for doubt because you have now practiced the technique and experienced it for yourselves, and so you know it. You will think, "Even in such a short time I am able to come out of suffering immediately to such an extent, but my strength is not yet exhausted." And the will to exert yourself still more arises, and you will become happy with a happiness of which you never tire.

Now, tell me. There is such a thing as a universal monarch in the world, isn't there?

D: Yes, sir, there is.

S: When the time is right for a universal monarch to arise, will no one notice this fact?

D: We don't know, sir.

S: About one hundred years before the universal monarch arises the good news goes around and a commotion takes place. Then all are setting their hopes and yearnings on the universal monarch. They are happy, and when he is born they rejoice.

What are the circumstances necessary for a universal monarch to arise?

D: Only when the "jewel of the wheel" arrives, sir, can someone become a universal monarch.

S: Yes, before the jewel of the wheel arises he is called the embryo universal monarch, but even then his authority, wealth, and power are considerable. Will he say, "Let the jewel of the wheel not arise; what I have got is quite enough for me!"?

D: No, sir, he won't.

S: And why not?

D: Because he wants to become still greater through the arising of the jewel of the wheel.

S: So, when will the jewel of the wheel come?

D: It will come at the right time, sir.

S: The jewel of the wheel arises due to the merit the embryo universal monarch has accumulated. But there are still duties for him, and having understood these duties and keeping them in mind, he has to fulfil them. Now say there is an embryo universal monarch. His merit is ripe, but he doesn't fulfil the duties that are the final cause for his becoming a universal monarch. Will the jewel of the wheel arise of its own accord?

D: No, sir, it will not arise by itself, I think. He will have to exercise himself further.

S: Now let's say you were the embryo universal monarch waiting for the jewel of the wheel to arise so that you will reign over the whole world. You will still have to practice further. You have to keep *sīla*. But would you say, "Well, I don't need the jewel of the wheel any more. I am quite satisfied with the riches and splendour I have attained"?

D: No, sir.

S: You will not give up at this point, because if you become a universal monarch you will be able to reign according to the Dhamma so that the whole world will be happy. Do you think the people of your provinces will say to you, "Oh embryo universal monarch, you have got enough power"?

D: No, sir, certainly not.

S: So, what will the people say?

D: "Work hard and fulfil your duties," they will say, sir.

S: And why is this?

D: Because they want the jewel of the wheel to arise, sir.

S: Yes, you see, because of the power of the wheel of the universal monarch, all will experience many different types of happiness. But when one has become a universal monarch, will this give him results for the rest of the cycle of birth and death? How long can he be universal monarch?

D: Only as long as the jewel of the wheel is there, sir.

S: Yes, even a universal monarch can be on his throne at best for one life span, but now the Buddha's teachings are available. If all the good beings who have taken birth in a happy existence take up the practice of the Buddha's teachings, they can attain awakening—as they aspired to in the past. But it is as with the embryo universal monarch: he doesn't become a universal monarch by just enjoying the royal splendour that he has already achieved; he will only become a universal ruler when he has fulfilled the duties and disciplines necessary to obtain the jewel of the wheel.

Now, approximately when do you want to attain Nibbāna?

D: Very soon, sir.

S: What does that mean?

D: Now, immediately, sir.

S: So, you are going to attain it right now?

D: If it's possible, sir.

S: Well, at the time you accept it, you will reach it.

D: One can get it only when the ten perfections (*pāramīs*) are completed, fulfilled, sir.

S: You still don't understand. We were talking about the embryo universal monarch just now. He attained that point because of his fulfilling the ten *pāramīs*. This fulfilment of the *pāramīs* means that he can become a universal monarch for certain. But when will he become a universal monarch? When he has fulfilled the practices and duties that cause the arising of the jewel of the wheel. So, if he undertakes these, the jewel will arise. Now, don't tell me you want Nibbāna. If you practice now, you will realize it now. Will you take up practicing? But then don't get up after some time and run away.

If you want to become sovereign rulers, what do you have to do? You have to master all the arts that are required of an accomplished prince and princess. So what do you think you have to master as sons and daughters of the Buddha?

D: We have to master *sīla*, *samādhi*, and *paññā*, sir.

S: What do you have to do to become a king? You have to study and practice the eighteen arts a king has to master. You have to learn about war-elephants, strategy, how to overcome enemies, and so forth. Once you have learned all this, what will you do when you encounter enemies?

D: We'll attack them, sir.

S: There are enemies who obstruct our progress towards Nibbāna, and if we want to get there, we have to fight them. Will you fight them after having equipped yourselves with weapons?

D: Yes, sir.

S: You will have to sit for a long time. Once the battle starts, you have to fight for real. Once you have deployed your troops in the battlefield, you will have to go ahead. Only if you prevail will you become a king.

D: We shall fight, sir.

S: Good, go ahead. Don't get up and run away, even if time seems long. If you fight well, you will become a sovereign king.

During the time of the Buddha, people learned the teachings from the Buddha himself. The Buddha simply taught how to defeat all forms of ignorance. Do you think that all those who listened to his words and then practiced accordingly repulsed ignorance? They really refuted all forms of ignorance and therefore they were victorious. They attained supreme happiness. Establish yourselves in effort and all your aspirations will be realized. You are well equipped with weapons for the battle, aren't you?

D: Yes, sir.

S: And you will fight, won't you? Your enemies do attack, and they attack often and with full force. Are sloth, torpor, and laziness friends or enemies? What do you do when they come? I think it has been some time since you fought a battle?

D: Quite some time, sir.

S: Tell me about the weapons you will have to use, and how you have to fight.

D: We have to fight for one hour every day, sir.

S: Only one hour a day?

D: We can't even always manage that much, sir.

S: Look here! Is this because the weapons are soft or because the warriors are soft?

D: We are soft, sir.

S: Are princes and princesses who want to become rulers soft too?

D: No, sir. They can't be because soft princes are defeated.

S: But these princes here, are they people with strength and fortitude or are they soft?

D: We are soft, sir.

S: As sons and daughters of the Buddha do you want to become sovereigns of Nibbāna, or do you want to remain princes and princesses?

D: We all want to become rulers, sir.

S: The weapon you have is good, so attack! But only if you hold the weapons properly will the enemy fear you. I think you don't hold the weapon properly.

D: We do attack, sir, but our way of attack is weak. Out of compassion give us a powerful weapon, sir.

S: I can only give you the weapon. This weapon will not do anything; only if you take this weapon and make use of it can you win. No weapon is weak, and you don't have just one. You have a whole store of weapons. If I were to enumerate them, it would become a long list.

D: Sir, we fail because we have so many weapons.

S: No, it's because you don't fight. You have to fight. Do you understand? Don't you want to become sovereign kings? Do you want to stay princes and princesses?

D: We try hard, sir, but we never succeed.

S: Yes, yes, but the weapon is all right. You don't succeed because you don't fight. You are talking like most people. You meditate, you put forth effort, but in spite of that you sound as if there was no effort. There is so much energy in you, but you don't use it. You do have energy. If you put all your stock of energy to use, you will assuredly become real sons and daughters of the Buddha, become kings by attaining Nibbāna. Sons and daughters of the Buddha have the ability to accept instructions, make effort, and follow the teachings of the Buddha. All who practice the teachings, be they humans, *devas*, or *brahmās*, can fulfil their different aspirations for Nibbāna. Even if you keep up the awareness of in-breath and out-breath throughout only one day, you will understand much. You may say that you have been meditating for so many years, but have you really ever been able to keep your mind focused for a full day?

D: No, sir.

S: By one day I mean a day and a night, twenty-four hours. Now, do this: practice the teachings of the Buddha to the full for one day and one night. If you have done this once, you will all be able to appreciate the value of just one single day. Some of you may have been practicing for twenty or thirty years and some even longer. But just examine yourselves. Have you really, having established yourselves in complete effort, fulfilled one single day in practice? Have you?

D: No, sir, we haven't.

S: And why have you never devoted yourselves fully for one whole day? You do have the energy required, don't you?

D: Yes, sir.

S: You don't use the energy you have in the right place. You waste it for no purpose. Are you still going to shows and entertainments?

D: Yes, sir. We watch a *pwe*[38] all night until dawn, without sleeping.

S: How many nights in a row do you do this?

D: About two or three nights, sir.

S: How many shows have you seen in all?

D: I can't remember, sir.

S: You see; there you have plenty of energy. Day and night. There your effort is strong. Now, how many times have you observed the Uposatha precepts?

D: Many times, sir.

S: I mean, how many days have you observed the eight Uposatha precepts day and night?

D: We have observed them ever since we were children, sir.

S: How many days altogether? A day I call a day and a night, twenty-four hours. Do you get a full day of Uposatha observances, if you look at it like this?

D: No, sir, we don't. We observe them about half a day at a time, sir.

S: Have you fulfilled them to the utmost during that half day?

D: We are unable to do that, sir. We started this morning, sir, and shall keep it up until tomorrow.

S: You do have the will to work, but you don't usually use it for this noble purpose, but rather to watch *pwes*. If you die while watching a *pwe*, where will you go?

D: To the lower world, sir.

S: Do you want that?

D: No, sir.

S: Even if you don't want it, it has great power over you, doesn't it? If you were to really observe the Uposatha day, with full effort for the whole day, could you not fulfil your aspirations? If you keep up the practice on an Uposatha day, you will understand, you will come to know something.

The real disciples of the Buddha take *sīla* on Uposatha days, and then they immediately take the object and firmly keep their attention fixed on it. Now if your attention is so firmly fixed on an object, can sloth, torpor, or laziness disturb you?

D: No, sir, they can't.

S: If our attention is firmly established on in-breath and out-breath and the point of contact, do we still hear other people's conversation?

D: No, sir.

S: What if someone speaks very loudly?

D: It doesn't disturb us, sir.

S: There is no greed, aversion, or delusion. If our minds are thus purged of greed, aversion, and delusion, will there still be loneliness, depression, and laziness?

D: No, sir.

S: Do we still miss company?

D: No, sir.

S: Do we still want to know what others are saying?

D: No, sir.

S: If someone comes and invites us out, are we excited?

D: No, sir.

S: We shall not jealously guard what we have. Good people are not like that. We share it with those with whom we live. "May they also get what I have got." Now, what will happen if all of you establish strong effort from sunrise to sunset, without a break. This is a long time-span, from sunrise to sunset. But will you feel it to be long?

D: No, sir.

S: You will think, "Today the time went so quickly! We observed Uposatha and the time just flew! And I really don't know why this day was so short." And after sunset you will again establish awareness of the object, and then day will break, and you still continue with the awareness of the spot below the nose, above the upper lip until it is light. Without interruption. And you will wonder, "How did this night pass so quickly? Now it is day again!"

This is how they used to practice on Uposatha days. When the direct disciples of the Buddha undertook to practice for a day, they practiced for twenty-four hours. And when day came, they were still not satisfied and said,

"In the long cycle of birth and death we have been doing all those other things for a long time, but not this." And they continued their work without wavering. Do you have days like this?

D: Our days contain some interruptions, sir.

S: If someone keeps Uposatha, and his mind wanders here and there—just anybody, I don't mean you—so his mind flits around here and there. But he is at a pagoda or under a holy Bodhi tree, and say he dies at that moment. What will happen to this worshipper?

D: He will go to the lower worlds, sir.

S: How many lower planes are there?

D: There are four lower planes, sir.

S: What are they?

D: Hell, the animal world, the plane of the hungry ghosts, and the demon world.

S: Now, who wants to go to hell or the animal world?

D: I don't, sir.

S: What about the ghost world or the demon world?

D: I don't want to go there, sir.

S: If you take *sīla* and don't firmly put your mind to observing the teachings of the Buddha, is that skilful or not?

D: It is unskilful, sir.

S: If someone observes the Uposatha days without keeping his mind focused, where will he be reborn when he dies?

D: In the lower planes of existence, sir.

S: Are you sure?

D: Yes, sir, I'm sure.

S: If I talk about someone who doesn't keep his mind fixed on the object, I am not talking about you people; I'm talking about that (fictional) worshipper.

D: Sir, out of compassion show us the good road out of the lower worlds.

S: Do you remember how you focused your mind as the Buddha taught?

D: Yes, sir, I remember.

S: So then, let us keep the mind on the spot. What do you think?

D: Yes, sir.

S: But, of course, now you can't do a full day any more. But if you practice until it is light, you will have done half a day. What do you think?

D: We will keep our minds at the spot, sir.

S: What other things do you have to do tonight?

D: There is nothing to do at night, sir.

S: You have eaten, so you don't have to cook any more, and there is nothing else to do. Very good. Will you stay here now that you have undertaken to keep the Uposatha days? Won't you want to go away?

D: We shall do our best, sir.

S: If you say, "We shall do our best," will there be no disturbances coming in? Will no enemy attack? Only if you really mean it are the enemies afraid. If you are firm, they run. You know about Mahā-Kassapa, don't you?

D: Yes, sir, we have heard about him.

S: He met the Buddha and then practiced what the Buddha taught in order to escape from suffering. There are four bodily postures: sitting, standing, walking, and lying down. Which of these is prone to let in the enemy? Laziness and sloth come in while lying down, and they come to stay, don't they? If we indulge in laziness and sloth, shall we be able to develop in morality, concentration, and wisdom?

D: No, sir, we won't.

S: Laziness and torpor are our enemies. Therefore Mahā-Kassapa rejected this posture in which the enemy attacks and adopted the other three postures in which the enemy can't remain for long.

There are thirteen ascetic practices and Mahā-Kassapa practiced all thirteen. Only those among the disciples of the Buddha with the strongest determination practiced the sitter's practice, that is, did not lie down at all, twenty-four hours a day. If one takes up the sitter's practice and makes the strong determination not to sleep, this sloth and laziness can't overpower him. Though these noble disciples of the Buddha did not lie down or sleep, they lived long and were very healthy.

Do you fight wars?

D: Yes, sir, we do.

S: Now, you are going to start your meditation. What preparations do you have to make?

D: We have to spread out our mat.[39]

S: If you spread out your mat before starting your meditation, soon someone will come along. Who do you think that will be? Do you think laziness and sleepiness will come your way?

D: If they come, sir, I shall lie down and sleep.

S: What will you say to them?

D: I won't say anything, sir.

S: You will say, "Ha, now only you come; I got the mat ready a long time ago." And what are you going to do then? You are going to lie down flat on your back and sleep. If you do this, will you be able to fulfil your aspiration for Nibbāna?

D: No, sir.

S: If you practice without sleeping, you are establishing full effort and are always keeping your attention firmly fixed on the object, day and night. If you practice in this way, your morality, your concentration and control over the mind, and your insight and wisdom will become stronger and stronger.

They will develop from moment to moment.

If you watch a *pwe* all night, you will feel tired in the morning. But if you practice the teachings of the Buddha all night, you will experience happiness and joy without end, and you will not feel sleepy. Do you understand? ... The Buddha taught this; it is not my teaching. If you follow the teaching of the Buddha and don't rest until you understand it completely, you will really know.

If people tell you, "This shade is cool," don't simply believe them, but try it out for yourselves. If you just repeat, "It is cool, it is cool …," because others say so, you don't really know about its coolness; you merely talk about it. If someone just babbles along, he doesn't show appreciation. But if someone speaks from experience, then won't he be able to speak with deep appreciation and radiant happiness and love?

So pay attention and practice. If you practice, you will reach your goal. Not just hundreds, not thousands, not tens of thousands, not hundreds of thousands; all who follow the teachings will master them.

When you start to meditate you still have to check: Is everything arranged? Is there a place to sleep at night and one to rest during the day? Only when all this is in order, will you meditate. Isn't that so?

If you act in this way, you nourish your enemy, you call him a friend; you love him. Once you recognize your enemy as such, do you still associate with him?

D: No, sir.

S: What do you do if he comes?

D: We check him and defend ourselves.

S: How do you defend yourselves? Will you attack him? Will you mount a full attack?

D: We shall repulse him, sir.

S: How do you repulse him? Softly, so that he doesn't get hurt?

D: We shall ward him off immediately so that he can never come back.

S: Yes, carry on. Cut him off and throw him overboard so that he can't ever come back. Well then, what will you do when tiredness and laziness really arise?

D: I shall probably fall asleep, sir.

S: What about others in the audience?

D: I don't know, sir.

S: Will you recognize the enemy and destroy him?

D: Just so, sir.

S: Very good. I shall give you a simile. If a man sleeps a deep sleep and you wake him up, he will awake quickly. If you try to wake up someone who pretends to sleep, you will not be successful. Why is this so?

D: The more one works on him the more he pretends to sleep.

S: Yes. Now what about you; are you really fast asleep or do you pretend to sleep?

D: I don't know, sir.

S: If you are really asleep, you will simply get up when I wake you up. Will you get up?

D: Yes, sir.

S: Yes, and after getting up, you will go back to sleep, I think. But I'm not sure about that. I only think so.

D: I shall work hard as you instruct me, sir.

S: Put forth effort and you will become perfect. You have all you need.

All of you have acquired the elements of insight and renunciation. Because of this, you now esteem the teachings of the Buddha; you want to fulfil and practice them. If the accumulation of the perfection of renunciation is small, your ears will be blocked to the teachings of the Buddha. For instance, if somebody tells you to come to this place, you don't want to come because you are bored by this. But now you are attracted by this teaching. All you need now is the same amount of effort that the noble disciples of the Buddha made.

When you begin to practice you may worry, "If I sit just for one or two hours, I am aching and stiff. How can I possibly sit for a whole day and night? I think that's quite impossible." Don't you worry like this?

D: No, sir, I don't.

S: Though you may not worry now, it will come up. But don't worry in this way. The Buddha didn't teach to suffer. He taught the way leading to happiness. You may not believe this because you think your own thoughts. But you have to work with full effort and without wavering. Now, when you meditate with full effort, the *viriya-iddhipāda* factor will arise. You will understand this. But when you sit, all of you feel some discomfort, don't you?

D: Yes, sir, we do.

S: Even if you are aching and stiff, there is a place where there is no pain. There is sleepiness, and there is also a place where there is no sleepiness. What do you do when you are drowsy?

D: I go to sleep, sir.

S: Do you ever get enough sleep?

D: Yes, sir, I do.

S: But you sleep every day, and now you want to sleep again? So you haven't actually had enough yet. If you sleep every day, you will never get enough sleep. So when you feel sleepy, make an effort to reach the place where there is no sleepiness, and then you will need no more sleep. Get up and walk up and down. Keep your attention at the spot where the air touches when you breathe in and out. If you keep it fixed on this spot with full effort, at some time you will find the place of no sleep. There is no "I won't find it," there is only a "I haven't got there yet." You will get it.

If you sleep and postpone meditation until you are rested, you will wake up when it is light and there will be no time left to meditate. I am just telling you what the Buddha taught. There is nothing I know. Everything the Buddha taught is true.

All of you have to make a living, work, toil, and shoulder burdens, don't you?

D: Yes, sir.

S: So let us be simple. You breathe, don't you?

D: Yes, sir, we do.

S: So, simply be aware of the in-breath, the out-breath, and the point below the nose where the air touches. It goes in and out without interruption, doesn't it?

D: Yes, sir, that's right.

S: Only when your attention wanders away is the continuity broken. And then, don't allow your attention to follow the breath. Your attention should always remain with this small spot. When you keep your attention there at the spot, your respiration will become soft and subtle. Once it has become subtle, you don't have to make it rough again. The Buddha taught that we have to make the rough and harsh subtle and fine. The Buddha didn't say that we should make the subtle rough. When you feel the spot, touching it with your finger, your attention will not wander to other objects. Can't you fix your attention firmly on the spot with the breathing?

D: I can, sir.

S: Will greed, aversion, and delusion still arise when your attention is focused on the spot? When you are well concentrated, even for a short moment, your mind is cleansed of greed, aversion, and delusion for that short moment. Can't you keep your attention fixed on the spot for a longer time-span?

D: Yes, sir, I can.

S: So, make a strong effort and keep your attention here. If you keep it there, is there any drowsiness or laziness disturbing you?

D: They don't come up, sir.

S: But what will happen if you reduce your effort?

D: Laziness will come in, sir.

S: Sloth and laziness will come, and your concentration will become weak. This is because you're at the beginning; later it will improve. And then you should view this laziness as a friend, not as an enemy, and you will get used to it. Though it comes, you will not get lazy any more. When we feel sleepy, we say, "This is good. Now I want to find the place where one doesn't feel sleepy quickly. Then there will be an end to sleeping." Work, fix your attention firmly on the spot as I just instructed you, and when your limbs ache, know: "The only way out of this is to get to a place where there is no pain." Now, if the discomfort becomes very intense, is it too difficult then?

It is not difficult. Don't worry about all this. Simply keep your attention on the spot. Put it back on the spot. Don't allow it to go away! If it runs away, you will never get to the place I just told you about.

Though we can't avoid being offered food and having to eat it, don't you think that we can keep our attention at the spot and eat? Do you think you will make comments like, "Too much salt, too little salt," about the food that your wife, daughter, granddaughter brought from home?

D: I wouldn't make that sort of comment, sir.

S: So, if they offered you food that was far too salty, would you become angry?

D: No, sir, I wouldn't.

S: Do you think you would even notice that the food had too much salt?

D: No, sir.

S: Why? Because you are aware of something far better, so you don't notice their food. If you get upset and angry about food, even though you are observing the eight precepts, and you die at that moment of anger, where will you go?

D: To the lower worlds, sir.

S: If you work with proper effort, not just superficially, will you even know whether the food tastes good or bad?

D: No, sir.

S: Keep your mind steadfastly focused on the spot. Your daily work needn't suffer. It doesn't cost you anything. Others won't know about it. Will you practice the sitter's practice tonight?[40] Keep your attention on the spot and you will find it very easy. If you feel drowsy, or if you are aching, say: "Good, it has come early," and then concentrate still harder on the spot.

If you reach the goal before drowsiness and discomfort come up, so much the better. If these disturbances don't manifest themselves, don't stop working, thinking, "If they don't even come up now, there is no need to work to get to a place where they don't exist." Just keep working.

Will you undertake the sitter's practice? Or will you, when sleepiness and tiredness set in, change to another (of the four) postures and reduce your effort?

D: We won't reduce our effort, sir.

S: All of you, or just a few among you?

D: All of us, sir.

S: So, if you keep each other company, so much the better. Now, then, undertake to carry out the sitter's practice!

I'll say it in Pāỵi, you repeat after me:

Seyyaṃ paṭikkhippami, nesajjikaṅgaṃ samādiyāmi.[41]

(I shall abstain from lying down. I undertake the sitter's practice.)

You may think, "It wasn't right that we just gave in to sleepiness in the past." Well, now you have undertaken the sitter's practice, and I think it is for the first time isn't it?

D: Yes, sir, the first time.

S: This is the weapon. With this weapon you can fight your battle. With this weapon you will be victorious. If you fight with a pillow as a weapon, you cannot win.

I shall tell you a story you probably already know. At the time of the Buddha, there was a rich lady who owned a big estate. When she became old, she distributed the inheritance among her children. But the children, after receiving the money, didn't care for their mother any more. She was not treated well in the houses of her sons and daughters and she was in distress.

When she was about eighty or ninety years old, the neighbours had her ordained as a nun (*bhikkhunī*),as they couldn't bear to see her poverty and suffering. When the nuns of her nunnery were invited for alms food to a house one day, they all went. Only Soṇā Therī,[42] our old woman, had to stay back because she was too old to go along.

Before they left the nunnery they said to Soṇā Therī, "You are very old, you can't come with us. But fill the water pots for drinking water, and those for washing hands and feet, so that everything is ready when we return, and also prepare some hot water."

But this nun was very old. To carry the water she had to use a small pot, and as she was working away, she got very tired. But she didn't rest. She forced herself to do what she had been ordered to do. Because she overworked herself, she fell down between the water pots, and couldn't lift herself up. She wasn't pretending; she was exhausted from carrying water.

She had been given the teachings of the Buddha. So she thought, "Well... I can't fill the pots any more. There is more water to be carried and I haven't prepared any hot water yet either. But I can't even get up. I will take up an object of meditation given by the Buddha." And she started meditating as we did. She fixed her attention firmly on the spot. She focused her attention so that it stayed there, whatever happened. That's all! And as she was meditating with strong effort, she did what had to be done and made an end to suffering.

Of course she was full of the bliss of emancipation. When the others came back, they couldn't find her. "Where could this old nun have gone?" they said and looked all over the nunnery. Eventually they found her lying between the water pots, and they all gathered around her and abused her. "Now what about our orders? You didn't fill the pots, and there is no hot water either. You are so lazy that you just lie down and sleep."

But the old nun was absorbed in bliss. The other nuns were worldlings, of course, and they stood there blaming her. “Look how lazy she is. No water pot is full, no hot water. Just lying around!”

You too can talk like that, can’t you? Not pleasant talk. But this nun was an Arahat. She had attained Arahatship along with the super-normal powers. She said: “All that you desire will be done. There will be water in the pots and there will be hot water too.” And after saying this, she made a strong determination, and the water pots were filled to the brim and the hot water was boiling over.

This nun was very old, and in exhaustion she fell down and could not get up again. She practiced as you are doing now. Do you hear this? How long will it take you to reach the goal, you who are healthy and strong?

D: We shall work hard.

S: Will you still say, “Oh, we are old; we can’t practice any more”? Soṇā Therī was eighty or ninety years old and she still carried the water as she had been told to do. When she fell down in exhaustion she just meditated. The disciples of Buddha attained the goal because their power of effort was great.

You have the teachings, the technique. All you need now is effort. And why do you need effort? Because during meditation the enemies will come to disturb you.

Keep your attention on this small spot. If your limbs ache, work so that you reach the state where there is no aching. When you are drowsy, work so that you reach the state where there is no drowsiness. Good, good … establish effort and meditate, work to make an end to all suffering.

Discourse Seven

To Light a Fire

Sayadaw: You have taken the moral precepts; now practice them. Only when your practice of morality (*sīla*) is perfect can you fulfil your aspirations for awakening. Having perfected yourselves in *sīla*, you have to perform various other meritorious practices, and these can take you to the pinnacle and the fulfilment of your aspirations.

The teachings of the Buddha are enshrined in the Tipiṭaka. These teachings were not given by the Buddha just to be preached and studied. You are good people; you have to practice the teachings with unwavering effort from the time you obtain them in order to escape from this suffering.

Do not get confused about the teachings. We don't have to know many techniques, only one; but that we should know clearly. If we establish one technique with strong effort and get rid of all doubts, then, without asking anyone else, we shall find the answers.

Choose one technique and practice it steadfastly. If you focus your mind at the small spot where the air touches when you breathe in and out, then there will be no greed, no aversion, no delusion, and as these three are absent, you are immediately out of suffering. So, for a short moment your mind is pure. Now, if your last mind-moment came up at this time and you died, would there be anything to be worried about or to be afraid of?[43]

The benefits accruing to you from this practice don't last for just a short moment or one lifetime. This short moment of purity will bring benefits for the remainder of the cycle of birth and death. And why can you accomplish this? Because the time is right, your form of existence is right, and you are putting forth right effort.

The disciples of the Buddha took the practice from the Teacher and worked with unwavering perseverance. Therefore, they achieved the awakening they had aspired for.

How did they work? In the same way as a man who wants to light a fire with a fire stick, as in the olden days. They rubbed two pieces of wood together, and heat was produced. Eventually the wood started to glow, and then they could light a fire. So, if a man wants to start a fire in this way and rubs two pieces of wood together does he count: "One rub, two rubs, three rubs …"?

Disciple: No, sir, that wouldn't work very well.

S: How would he have to do it then?

D: He would have to rub continuously until he got a flame.

S: Yes, when they wanted to start a fire in those days, this was the only way to do it. They had to rub with strong determination and without taking breaks. Now, if one were to rub two pieces of wood together in this way, how long would it take for the fire to start?

D: When it gets hot enough, the fire will start, sir.

S: Will that take long?

D: Not very long, sir.

S: No, if this man works with determination, it doesn't take long. It is just the same with this practice here. You want fire. You know that if you rub these two pieces of wood together you can have it. Now, if you count, "One rub, two rubs …" it will become a little hot. And then you take rest for a while. Will you start a fire?

D: No, sir.

S: Okay, so you start again, once, twice, three times … and again heat is produced. Then you lay back again and take a bit of rest. Will you start a fire?

D: No, sir.

S: And if you continue in this way for a whole month?

D: We won't get fire.

S: And if you continue for a whole year?

D: It will just get warm, sir, but there will be no fire.

S: Now, what if you were to work like this for one hundred years?

D: It will just become warm, sir.

S: In that case, there is no fire in these two pieces of wood?

D: There is fire, sir, but the effort and perseverance are not sufficient.

S: It is just the same with our work. You have to work as the fire maker does, without taking rest. Soon it will become hot and then, before long, a fire will start.

Only then will you be able to use the fire in the way you want. You should all make the effort to fulfil your aspiration for awakening. You have received the teachings of the Buddha. Now you have to work so that your efforts are equal to the efforts of those wise men of old who attained their goal. The teachings of the Buddha are the only path out of suffering, and you can practice them only when a Buddha has arisen, and as long as his teachings are available. When a Buddha's teachings are unavailable, you cannot fulfil your aspiration for Nibbāna. But when a Buddha arises in the world, he expounds right conduct (*caraṇa*) and understanding (*vijjā*), which lead out of suffering. If you use the opportunity and put them into practice, you will become perfect. Right conduct can also be practiced when there are no teachings of a Buddha, but insight or understanding is not available.

What exactly does right conduct mean? Now that the teachings of a Buddha are available, all of you untiringly give the four requisites of food, robes, shelter, and medicine to the monks. When you give, you offer the best you can afford. But still you are not satisfied yet; you want to do more and more. This is good conduct (*caraṇa*)?

To practice the teachings of the Buddha to the point of being able to escape from all suffering, we have to be aware of one single object continuously, without break or interruption. If we are thus aware, we are practicing understanding (*vijjā*). Practicing both together and being perfect in effort, the wise men of old attained to the awakening to which they aspired.

You may think, "Well, we make offerings to the teachings by giving food, clothing, shelter, and medicine to the monks. To realize the teachings for ourselves we would have to practice insight. We shall do that if we have some free time after preparing our offerings." Now if you work like this, are you practicing right conduct or insight?

D: It is right conduct, sir.

S: When you have fulfilled your duties and keep your mind steadfastly focused on one single object, what are you practicing then?

D: Wisdom, sir.

S: So, what happened to right conduct? When you keep your attention focused on the spot, are you still practicing right conduct?

D: Yes, sir, then we are practicing right conduct (*caraṇa*) and understanding (*vijjā*) at the same time.

S: Yes, you can practice the two jointly. First you prepare food and then you meditate. Thus we have to perfect ourselves in both practices, in right conduct and understanding. But you practice right conduct first, and only then do you practice understanding. Is it not possible to practice these emancipating teachings of the Buddha simultaneously? Is it not possible to be aware of the in-breath and the out-breath even while preparing food or while building a monastery?

D: It's possible, sir.

S: You see, this is the way the wise disciples of the Buddha used to practice. They had the ability to accept good advice and instructions. Do you think they might have thought, "Our parents, who are our highest possessions and to whom we owe an infinite debt of gratitude, are getting old. We have to serve them day and night, therefore we can't meditate"?

D: Sir, some must have thought in this way.

S: Is the fulfilment of one's duties towards parents included in right conduct or in understanding?

D: It is right conduct, sir.

S: Isn't it possible to be aware of mind and matter while you look after your parents?

D: It's possible, sir.

S: Now that you know that the wise men of old practiced right conduct and understanding simultaneously, do you still consider it impossible to practice understanding while serving your children and grandchildren? Can't you train your mind in the awareness of mind and matter at the same time that you are fulfilling all your duties? Wherever you are, whatever you do, you can practice right conduct and meditation at the same time. When your children are good, you can be aware of the in-breath and out-breath, and when they are naughty and you have to correct them, then too you can practice. Tell me, what element of the training is your correcting the children?

D: It is right conduct, sir.

S: So, if you practice awareness while scolding them, what are you practicing?

D: Understanding, sir.

S: If we practice awareness while we do what we have to do, will we suffer? Does it cost us anything? Does it disturb our work?

D: No, sir. If one works with awareness the work is completed more quickly.

S: If you don't allow yourselves to be distracted, you will work faster, and you will earn more money. Your aspiration to Nibbāna too will be fulfilled more quickly. All the beings who practice in this way can fulfil their aspirations. There is not a single second in which it isn't possible to fulfil your aspiration. How about those human beings, *devas*, and *brahmās* who don't practice the teachings of the Buddha, though the time is good? Do they attain the fulfilment of their aspirations?

D: Those who don't make effort can't fulfil their aspirations, sir.

S: Why? Is it because they aren't reborn in the right plane of existence or because it isn't the right time?

D: No, sir, but without effort nothing can be accomplished.

S: Maybe they don't have sufficient *pāramīs*?

D: Maybe some can't grasp the teachings because they haven't completed their perfections sufficiently in the past, sir.

S: But if you don't put forth effort, can you still claim that you don't understand because of missing *pāramīs*?

D: Those who have accumulated perfections in the past attain the stages of Nibbāna when they listen to the teachings. But we, sir, because we have no perfections, we listen to the Dhamma again and again, and we remain just the same.

S: The wise men of old were just like thirsty people. They were thirsty, so they looked for water. And when they found it, what did they do? Did they look up at the sky and say, "Well, we don't want to drink this water yet"? No, they were people who were really thirsty. What about you? You have the teachings of Buddha, do you drink them right away?

D: Sir, we linger and wait.

S: In that case it isn't true that you don't have any *pāramīs*. If you don't drink, your thirst will not be quenched. What will you do if you find yourselves sitting right next to the water pot?

D: Because we don't have a sufficient amount of *pāramī*, we just sit there, sir.

S: What will you do if you walk into a lake full of water?

D: When we walk down into the water we stretch out our neck and turn our face up towards the sky, sir. And if we should dive, sir, we shall keep our mouth firmly shut.

S: Now, are you still telling me that you are thirsty, but that you don't have the necessary understanding to be able to drink?

D: Sir, because we don't have the necessary conditioning, we don't open our mouth in the water.

S: If you really wanted to drink, would you still keep your mouth shut?

D: If one really wanted to drink, one wouldn't, of course.

S: So you are saying, "Though I do want to drink, I do not want to drink!" Aren't you contradicting yourselves?

D: It is as if we pretended not to want to drink, sir.

S: Tell me then, if you are thirsty and just bear it, are you happy or unhappy?

D: Unhappy, sir.

S: So, if you are unhappy, will you keep sitting near the water pot without drinking?

D: Sir, we see this kind of suffering as happiness.

S: Did the Buddha teach that this thirst is happiness?

D: No, sir, he said it was suffering.

S: Now, tell me, what do you think is true, what the Buddha said or what you think?

D: Our view, that this is happiness, is wrong, sir.

S: Do you want to be happy or unhappy?

D: Though we would like to be happy, we continue to create unhappiness for ourselves.

S: What is better, to listen to the Buddha or not to listen to the Buddha?

D: Sir, we know that we should follow the word of the Buddha, but still we continue to create suffering for ourselves.

S: In that case it seems as if you knew your own good, but that you are simply lazy.

D: Because our *pāramīs* are weak, we have to suffer from our own ignorance, sir.

S: Now, if there is water and you don't quench your thirst with it, is that because you have not perfected your *pāramīs*?

D: It is because of the lack of perfections that the power of ignorance is so overwhelming, sir.

S: Tell me, what is more powerful, understanding (*vijjā*) or ignorance (*āvijjā*)?

D: Sir, understanding is more powerful for human beings.

S: Then you know that the understanding the Buddha taught is powerful.

D: Sir, we know that understanding is a good thing.

S: So, just associate yourselves with understanding. Whether you think that the power of ignorance is strong or whatever … You have learned now to distinguish between mind and matter. While you are aware of mind and matter in the way the Buddha taught, is there still ignorance prevailing?

D: While we are aware, sir, there is no ignorance.

S: Now, let us concentrate at the spot below the nose above the upper lip with the awareness of mind and matter (*nāma* and *rūpa*), just as the Buddha taught. When we anchor our attention thus, can ignorance stay? If you look out for it, will you be able to find it?

D: It will be completely gone, sir.

S: Are you still aware when it has gone?

D: Sir, it has disappeared completely.

S: In that case, is the power of understanding greater or that of ignorance?

D: The power of ignorance is great, sir.

S: Oh dear, how is it great? The poor thing just ran as fast as it could; you couldn't even see it any more.

D: But it comes back again and again, sir.

S: This is so because you allow it back in. If you allow only understanding and knowledge in, ignorance can't come back. But if you allow it back, then slowly your understanding will break up and ignorance takes over once more. It is like the electric lights in here. What do you need to switch on the lights?

D: Switches, sir.

S: What happens inside the switches so that we get light?

D: Electricity flows through them, sir.

S: What happens if the flow is interrupted?

D: It will become dark, sir.

S: What do you have to do to turn the darkness into light?

D: We have to feed electricity to the bulbs, sir.

S: And where does the darkness go when the lights are lit?

D: It disappears, sir.

S: Is any of the darkness left behind?

D: No, sir.

S: When understanding shines, is there any ignorance left?

D: No, sir.

S: In that case, is the power of ignorance great?

D: No, sir, it isn't.

S: Is it difficult to do what we did just now?

D: Not very difficult, sir.

S: Don't we see the reality when light suddenly comes?

D: We do, sir.

S: Will you still be able to go wrong?

D: No, sir.

S: It is so easy! What did the wise disciples of the Buddha connect? If you want to switch on the light, you have to connect the wires inside the switch so that electricity flows. So, gently keep your attention on the spot; it will connect. Do you understand?

D: We would like to give this up, sir.

S: Just concentrate your attention there. Gently. Do you become tired if you focus your mind in this way?

D: No, sir.

S: Does it cost you anything?

D: No, sir.

S: Do you have to stop your work?

D: No, sir.

S: Isn't this wonderful? You can practice in all the four postures: sitting, standing, walking, and lying down. Can you keep your attention at the spot with the awareness of the in-breath and out-breath even while you are eating, drinking, and working?

D: Please, sir, teach us how to be aware of the breath while we are moving about and working.

S: You know about many different techniques, but you don't have to practice them all. Choose one and work with it. If you keep your mind steadfastly focused on one object, you will immediately be aware of what you have not been aware of before, just as you see light as soon as you turn on the switch. Can there still be wrong view and delusion in your mind while you are thus aware?

D: No, sir, but as we don't know where the light switches are, we have to remain sitting in the dark.

S: Oh dear, you've got so many switches! Whichever you turn on, the light will come.

D: Sir, because there are so many switches, I don't know which one to turn on.

S: Any one will do; the results will be immediate.

D: When I press that switch, sir, the light bulb immediately burns up. That's why I thought it was the wrong switch.

S: It doesn't burn up; it will light the bulb. Even if it shorts out one day; when you try again, it will certainly burn.

D: But I don't know where to press the switch, sir.

S: You know the switches; you have been taught so many techniques by the monks who have compassion for you. Now, do not try them all. Select one only.

D: Sir, please teach us this one technique!

S: Every technique the Buddha taught will work as a switch to turn on the light.

D: We would like to learn a technique by which we can perfect our conduct and train ourselves in understanding while we work, walk, or sit, sir.

S: Well then, tell me: do not all of you, big and small, breathe?

D: Yes, sir, we do.

S: So, there is no one here who doesn't know how to breathe. Can you say sometimes, "Sorry, I am very busy now. I don't have time to breathe"?

D: No, sir.

S: So then, it is very easy for you to breathe, isn't it? Now just try to find out where the air comes out when you breathe out.

D: It comes out of the nose, sir.

S: Is there any other place where it comes out?

D: No, sir, there is only one place.

S: Yes, there is only one place. So, don't come and tell me that there are so many switches that you don't know which one to press. You are all breathing, aren't you? Where does this air touch when you breathe out?

D: It touches at a point at the base of the nose, sir.

S: What happens when the air enters? Where does it touch?

D: It touches again there, at the same spot, sir.

S: So, this is quite obvious to you: The air brushes over a small spot at the base of the nose as you breathe in and out. You are aware of this, aren't you?

D: Yes, sir.

S: Don't allow the mind to wander away to other objects. Can you feel the spot where the air touches just as if you were touching it with your finger? Put your attention there and keep it there. Don't follow the breath outside the nostrils. Keep your attention quietly and calmly at the spot, and you will be able to know how the air goes in and out. The flow of air is continuous, isn't it?

D: Yes, sir, it is.

S: You can be aware of it without the slightest interruption. If you keep your attention there, there is only the awareness of mental properties and physical properties (*nāma* and *rūpa*). Now under which of the two do the nostrils come, under mind or under matter?

D: Sir, as far as I know, the nostrils are matter.

S: What is the entity that knows the touch sensation?

D: Sir, that which knows is mind (*nāma*).

S: So you are aware of mind and matter at the same time. If you are aware of mind and matter, are there still some more other entities of which you aren't aware?

D: No, sir, there is nothing apart from mind and matter.

S: Is being aware of mind and matter ignorance or knowledge?

D: It is knowledge, sir.

S: If one has no awareness of mind and matter, what do we call that?

D: That we call ignorance, sir.

S: Can ignorance still influence us while we are training ourselves in understanding?

D: No, sir, it can't.

S: Is there still cause for worry and fear about the present and the future?

D: No, sir, there isn't.

S: Even if you are aware for just one short moment, you benefit. How much will you receive if you can keep up this awareness for a longer period?

D: The benefits must be many, sir.

S: Will there still be doubt in your mind about your own ability to attain the awakening to which you have aspired?

D: No, sir.

S: You can reach your goal even quicker than you thought. Of course you still have to fulfil your duties towards your teachers, parents, and children. You have to support the teachings of the Buddha. You have to make a living. If you don't fulfil all these duties, is your *sīla* perfect?

D: It isn't, sir.

S: If your moral conduct isn't perfect, can you attain your goal?

D: No, sir, it is impossible.

S: Tell me: When or where is it not possible to practice right conduct and meditation simultaneously?

D: It is never too difficult, sir, even if one is ill.

S: If your insight develops through your practice, do you still need to tell others that you have become happy through the Buddha-Dhamma?

D: It isn't necessary to tell others, sir.

S: And if you don't talk about it, does it mean that you don't know about your own happiness?

D: Even if we don't tell everyone, we still know for ourselves, sir.

S: In just the same way noble people know. You know for yourselves how much you have got now, and when you reach the goal, then you will know. If you write on a piece of paper that salt is salty and someone reads this, he knows that salt is salty, doesn't he?

D: Of course, sir.

S: And if you just tell someone that salt is salty, will he know?

D: Why, certainly, sir.

S: But tell me, will salt become salty just by your writing so or saying so?

D: No, sir, of course not.

S: If you read that salt is salty, do you actually know that this is so?

D: Though one understands that it is salty, one doesn't actually know how salt tastes. Only if we put some salt on our tongue and taste it shall we actually know what "salty" means.

S: If you have tasted it and know it is salty, do you still have to read about it? Do you still have to make declarations about its taste?

D: No, sir.

S: If we tell our neighbour about its taste, will he know then?

D: He will just have heard about it, sir.

S: What do we have to do to make him know?

D: We have to give him some salt and make him taste. Otherwise, what he knows is just hearsay, sir.

S: Do you know for sure that right conduct and insight and wisdom constitute the path to the release from suffering?

D: Yes, sir, we know.

S: If you read that salt is salty and consider this knowledge to be quite sufficient, then that is where you stop. But if you want to make sure, you have to taste for yourselves. Is it sufficient to read that salt is salty and then have this confirmed by me?

D: Sir, you wouldn't lie. If you tell me it is salty, that is quite sufficient for me.

S: Now you are going back on what you said earlier. You know salt is salty from hearing and reading about it, but only if you really know for yourselves will you become happy. If you tell somebody that salt is salty and he blindly accepts what you say, then he won't even feel the desire to taste for himself. After all, he thinks he knows. With this notion in mind, he won't see the need to taste it. It is not easy to know for oneself that salt is salty. Salt does exist. Take it, taste it. Then you will know for yourselves and there will be no need to ask others.

D: Sir, yesterday I did taste a little bit of salt.

S: Really? Why only a little? Did the salt run out?

D: No, sir, there is plenty of it.

S: Then take it! Don't just taste a little bit. Use as much as you need. Every single one of you has got some salt, haven't you?

D: Yes, sir. We haven't eaten our full yet, sir, but we are satisfied with tasting just a little.

S: But, of course, you are not thinking of leaving it at that, are you?

D: Well, sir, not actually, but as time goes by everything changes. We planned something last year and already a year has passed …

S: Now, this time, don't merely think. How many "thinkers" were there at the time of the Buddha?

D: They were as numerous as grains of sand on the beach, sir.

S: You still have to make effort and meditate. You still have to strive to understand the teachings of the Buddha. You are planning to do that, aren't you? Will you only think about putting forth effort in this life also?

D: If we only think about it, sir, we shall again be left behind in the cycle of birth and death.

S: Now then, there is no problem. "In the past we missed out because we were only thinking about making effort, but now we know that there is fire in the two pieces of wood. We shall rub them together." Thinking in this way, there will be effort and also the desire to fight the battle … Have you got hold of the two pieces of wood? If I continue talking, you will think, "This monk is talking for a long time." I shall stop now. Only if you work can you make an end of it.

If you have the desire to work, then meditate, work hard, apply yourselves with the same effort and determination as did the Noble Ones of old.

Discourse Eight

A Happiness That Ever Grows

Webu Sayadaw:[44] Be perfect in the practice of *sīla*. Only if your practice is perfect will all your aspirations of the present time and of the future be fulfilled without exception. Because this is true, the aspirations of the good people of the past who practiced and strove were fulfilled completely. You too have to take up the practice of that *sīla* that brought about their happiness. Work hard and perfect yourselves in it.

Being perfect in *sīla*, keep your mind straight and practice generosity (*dāna*) as it pleases you, giving your possessions yourselves with sincerity to those who are worthy. Approach and give your offerings and your respect to the peerless Buddha and his teaching, keeping in mind your aspiration for awakening, Nibbāna. This type of aspiration is called right aspiration. What you realize when you penetrate the Four Noble Truths is called *bodhi*.

There are different types of *bodhi*: *sammā-sambodhi* (Buddhahood), *pacceka-bodhi* (Non-teaching Buddhahood), *sāvaka-bodhi* (Arahatship). There are different types of Arahatship: *agga-sāvaka* (chief discipleship), *mahā-sāvaka* (leading discipleship), *pakati-sāvaka* (simple discipleship as an Arahat). You have always to keep in mind your aspirations for Nibbāna, the highest goal.

Aspirations thus taken are well taken. After having perfected yourself according to your aspiration, attain Nibbāna. The noble persons who have attained Nibbāna are innumerable. Why could they bring their various aspirations for *bodhi* to fruition? Because they had been born into the right form of existence at the right time and because they exerted proper effort.

When is the time that these aspirations can be brought to fruition? From the moment the Buddha attained awakening, many human beings, *devas*, and *brahmās* came to the Buddha to pay respects and to show their devotion. But no human being, no *deva*, and no *brahmā* was satisfied by merely being in the presence of the Buddha and having the opportunity to pay respects. The Buddha observed them through his mind's eye and taught them the truth that he had penetrated through his own super-knowledge, his omniscience. As soon as they received the instructions of the Buddha, they began to practice, to exert themselves with unwavering energy in all the four postures of the body. This effort, which is continuous without break or pause and full of joy, is called good effort. When their effort was perfect and equal to the effort of the wise men of old, they arrived at their goal in due time and all the aspirations of their hearts came to an end. Because they had achieved this state they were exceedingly happy and blissful.

What was the nature of their happiness, their bliss? It was not happiness or bliss that lasted for only a moment or a single lifetime; it was that happiness that is so great it is able to last for the remainder of *saṃsāra*. Even if you are born in the human plane for only one life, you are able to rise above the suffering of the cycle of birth and death.

In this way happiness and bliss come to you. When one has attained this happiness, when one has received the sign of bliss, when one has reached the goal, there is no jealous guarding of a secret. No, you will want all human beings, *devas*, and *brahmās* to attain this bliss and happiness. As you know for yourself how to attain this happiness, the actions of body, speech, and mind will always be in harmony with the cause of attaining Nibbāna. You will act with joy as your base.

How could so many human beings, *devas*, and *brahmās* attain such high states of bliss? Only because they knew that they were going to bring the aspirations of their heart to fruition.

What are the things that support the Buddha's teachings? They are the donation of shelter, robes, alms food, and medicine for the monks. Having understood this, they practiced it. With these four requisites the wise supported the teachings of the Buddha. While they supported the teachings of the Buddha by donating the four requisites, many human beings *devas*, and *brahmās* received the instructions of the Buddha. They were endowed with the ability to understand and follow the instructions and they practiced with a joyful mind without taking rest as the wise of old. When they thus practiced they attained their goal without delay. In just one moment innumerable human beings, *devas*, and *brahmās* fulfilled the wish of their heart. The energetic people saw this and supported the teachings of the Buddha and established them in a very short time. But they didn't do only this; this didn't satisfy them yet. In order to strengthen and make firm the teachings they would also meditate. So they were full of good volition, and they were accordingly endowed with unwavering effort and faith. Since the time of the Buddha there have been such noble people who supported and carried out the teachings of Buddha with supreme effort, and ever since the days of the Buddha human beings, *devas*, and *brahmās* have been attaining Nibbāna. The number of those who have reached the goal in just a short moment can't be reckoned, let alone the number of all who have attained Nibbāna.

Now the good time for all the various noble people has come. This is so because the time when a Buddha and his teachings blossom is the good time. The existences of human beings, *devas*, and all the happy abodes are good. Having been born into one of these, people accepted the teachings as you are doing now. They practiced with full effort and arrived at the goal.

After his awakening the Buddha honoured Rājagaha before any other country with his presence. The king of this great city, Bimbisāra, came to the Buddha and because he received the teachings and followed them, he attained the goal. He was full of bliss. He wanted others to attain the same bliss, and understanding the reason, the cause for his happiness, he donated the four requisites. He did this so that his mother, father, grandmother, and grandfather could fulfil their aspirations completely. The Buddha, out of his great compassion, dwelt in the king's delightful garden. Humans, *devas*, and *brahmās* came to revere him there and with great compassion he taught them what he had realized himself. In just one short moment innumerable humans, *devas*, and *brahmās* achieved their aspirations. And after this it went on and on. The good time for all the people with noble aspirations had come! The time at which there is a Buddha or his teaching is the good time. Human life, life as a *deva* or a *brahmā*, is a good life. Good effort is called the effort that is established after one has received the teachings. And what are the Buddha's teachings? Everything in the Tipiṭaka preached and explained by noble disciples out of loving kindness and compassion is the Buddha's teaching. They are very extensive, profound, and difficult to understand. Though they are extensive, profound, and difficult to understand, they really are just one thing: the way of escape from suffering.

They are expounded by the wise in brief and in full as time permits, and everyone has knowledge of them according to his capability. You all have some understanding of the Tipiṭaka in accordance with your capabilities. If you were to talk about what you know it would never end.

But you have to establish strong effort and focus your mind on one object according to the teachings of the Buddha, as I said, and keep out all other objects. When you fix your mind on one object exclusively with strong and stable effort, then you will be established in the teachings. Isn't that so?

U Ba Khin: Yes, sir.

S: To establish your attention thus is effort (*viriya*). When you fix your attention on one object and no other object enters your mind and your attention is stable, you reach *viriya-iddhipāda.*[45] Because the teachings are so extensive you may think it tiresome to practice them. That is why I instruct you in this way, that you can reach the goal quickly.

What happens to the causes of suffering—*lobha*, *dosa*, and *moha* (greed, aversion, and delusion)—when you control your mind in this way?

U: They are cut out and become quiet.

S: People write and preach a lot about greed, aversion, and delusion, don't they? When they debate, they talk only to win the debate, whoever they are talking to. But if they establish awareness of breathing and make their minds stable, they acquire real merit. Why don't we try to do this?

U: Yes, sir.

S: Will there be worry, fear, and greed at that time?

U: There won't be.

S: No, there won't; there won't be any worry, fear, or greed. If there is worry, fear, or greed, are you happy or unhappy?

U: Unhappy, sir.

S: And if there is no worry, fear, or greed?

U: Then one is happy.

S: If one establishes effort only for one split second the *viriya-iddhipāda* arises. It excludes worry, fear, and greed, and there is happiness. There are types of happiness which are not related to the happiness achieved through the Buddha's teachings, but people still call them happiness. What sort of happiness am I talking about? I am talking about the happiness of becoming a human being or *deva*, of becoming a king, a rich man, a universal monarch, a *deva* king, a Sakka, or a *brahmā*. Of course their enjoyment is also called happiness … But let me give an example. If you were asked to bear the golden royal insignia and live in the golden palace of a country that abounded with gold, silver, gems, rice, water, and paddy, that was plentiful in everything, would you accept this offer or not?

U: Of course I would accept.

S: Of course you would accept. This country is so rich that there is absolutely nothing missing. So you would live wearing your crown in your golden palace smiling all the time. So I think, smiling like that all the time, you would enjoy yourself; you would be happy, wouldn't you? Would this happiness keep worry, fear, and wanting away?

U: No, it wouldn't.

S: Oh, really?

U: It wouldn't, sir.

S: I mean at that moment, you see.

U: It wouldn't.

S: Why are they all smiling and happy then?

U: Somebody could try to usurp the kingdom. If something happens in his territory he would have duties to fulfil.

S: There is nothing like that. This country is so good that there is no danger or worry of that kind. It is a very peaceful country. There is no problem at all; everything is calm and quiet. It is that kind of country. No troubles at all; you just have to live in the golden palace wearing your crown. You simply live there with your ministers, troops, concubines, and wives. You live always with a smile on your face. Will worry, fear, greed, and anxiety be kept at bay in these circumstances? You are always smiling and happy. So, do you think there is any worry?

D: There will be, sir.

S: Why?

D: Because there is the fear of death.

S: Yes, there will still be the fear of death. But you are smiling still. What is this smiling? What are greed, aversion and delusion?

U: They won't be kept away.

S: Even smiles don't keep them away?

U: No, sir.

S: What do smiles mean?

U: They indicate that the object of mind is *lobha* (greed).

S: Really? Is one happy if there is *lobha*?

U: No, sir.

S: Is *lobha* cool and pleasant?

U: No, it isn't.

S: Is it *kusala* (skilful) or *akusala* (unskilful)?

U: It is *akusala*.

S: Are you happy when you are smiling as we just said?

U: No, sir.

S: But you are smiling great smiles, aren't you? But you aren't happy yet. You are king, aren't you? Maybe you aren't happy because you rule only one country? I'll give you another one. So?

U: Even then I won't be any happier.

S: Are you going to tell me that you don't want another country?

U: No, sir, I would take it.

S: You would take it, but still not be happy. Well, I won't give you just another country; I'll give you the whole continent. Will you tell me that you don't want it?

U: No, sir.

S: So, will you be happier then?

U: I won't be happier.

S: Really? All right, I won't give you just another continent, but the whole planet and the jewel of the wheel of the universal monarch. Now, there won't be any worry or fear. With the turning of the jewel of the wheel you will become a universal monarch. Will you be happy now?

U: I won't, sir.

S: Will you feel calm and cool?

U: I won't.

S: Why not, disciple?

U: There is still the burning of greed, aversion and delusion?

S: Oh, is it still there?

U: It's still there.

S: So you aren't happy yet. Well now, what about Sakka, the *brahmās*, and the *deva* kings?

U: The same applies to them too.

S: We said they were happy and now you tell me the contrary?

U: The objects of their minds are greed, aversion and delusion?

S: Oh really? Let it be. If one lives to a ripe old age always smiling and then dies smilingly, will he find peace in the cycle of births and deaths?

U: He won't find peace.

S: Where will this smiling fellow go?

U: When the (good) *kamma* of this smiling person comes to an end, his fate will turn.

S: Yes, and where will this smiling fellow end up?

U: Because of his smiling, the mind will be controlled by greed and he is destined for the lower worlds.

S: Oh really … I thought that being happy was good, disciples. Is it not good? I have to ask you, "Is it good?"

U: (Laughing) No, it isn't.

S: Okay, we are not happy yet. But when I asked whether we would be happy later on, you said no. There was no peace, you said.

U: There is no peace.

S: So, now there is no peace; what about later? Will it become just a little bit better?

U: It won't improve, sir.

S: What will happen, in the lower planes …

U: We will go to the lower planes.

S: Really? So, there is no peace now; there won't be any after. Which is worse?

U: It will be worse later.

S: Oh … We all thought we were quite all right, but not so. But now we've got the teachings of the Buddha and we can have as much of it as we want, can't we?

U: We can.

S: Endowed with the ability to accept the teachings we can take up one technique with steadfastness. Will the happiness that derives from this practice become less the more we use it, the more we practice?

U: It won't.

S: Will it ever be exhausted?

U: It won't.

S: Oh, really? My word, this thing is good. Isn't it, my dear disciples? And if we use it all the time, continuously, will it then get used up, will it come to an end?

U: It will neither diminish nor get used up.

S: Wait a minute. We shall keep our attention focused while we are sitting like this, but while we are standing, can we still practice this?

U: We can.

S: And when we are walking?

U: We can.

S: Yes, we have to carry the burden of our body. It is not the same as other worldly possessions. When you work hard to acquire various jewels and gold and are successful, you will store them away in a certain place, I think. But having acquired our body and mind, the five *khandhas*, is it possible to live with ease, happily and without making great efforts?

U: It isn't possible.

S: We have to shoulder our burden. We can't rest for a short moment even, can we? And for whom do we have to shoulder the burden of our bodies without ever taking rest?

U: For ourselves.

S: For the five aggregates.

U: For the five aggregates, sir.

S: Yes, we have to work, disciples. If I practice this awareness a lot, then I don't want to miss the happiness that derives from it. Isn't it possible to practice this all the time?

U: It is possible, sir.

S: This is very good. Will it diminish?

U: No, sir, it won't.

S: Is it tiresome to keep up this awareness?

U: It isn't tiresome.

S: Will you use up material goods you have saved up?

U: No, sir.

S: You won't. What about your work; will it be disturbed?

U: It won't be disturbed.

S: Will others know about our practice?

U: They won't notice.

S: Oh, the other people won't notice? Yes, disciple, when we have the teachings of the Buddha and practice them continuously, when we are able to focus our mind on the object, we won't get tired, will we?

U: We won't, sir.

S: We won't spend anything; our work won't be disrupted, and others won't even notice. You receive the teachings in no time and then you say to yourself, "Now I shall follow these teachings." When you have this volition and put forth effort then the *viriya-iddhipāda* factor will arise and you will arrive at the goal in no time. If you take up the practice now, will your progress be slow or fast, my disciples?

U: According to circumstances, sir, sometimes it will be slow, sometimes …

S: No! Wait, wait …

U: Yes, sir.

S: Never mind about this. If I focus my attention according to the teachings and keep it with the awareness of respiration, isn't this much possible?

U: It is possible.

S: Is this quick or slow?

U: It is quick, sir.

S: You see. If you establish effort, the *viriya-iddhipāda* factor arises. Can you say how quick this is?

U: Yes, sir.

S: Have you put your attention there and does it stay?

U: Yes, sir.

S: As I decide to put it there, it stays, doesn't it?

U: It does.

S: So if it stays, you have reached happiness. Are you able to speak as quickly as this happiness is able to arise?

U: I am not, sir.

S: It is easy to achieve happiness if you want it.

U: Yes, sir.

S: This is the highest sort of *kusala*. Do you hear? This is the highest, the highest. Only if you have *pāramī* can you be born as a human and receive the Buddha-Dhamma. This type of *kusala* cannot be put in numbers. Do you understand? Then, the six qualities of the Dhamma are there; the qualities of the Buddha, the Dhamma, and the Saṅgha. When the Buddha taught this, people understood. Among the six qualities of the Dhamma, *akāliko* is one, isn't it? What does *akāliko* mean?

U: Immediateness.

S: Immediateness means that as soon as you fix your attention the results come. So, if you establish effort with intelligence the results come so quickly that you can't say "there" quicker than they come. Or you can't even think that fast. Is it so? If you establish awareness now, if you keep it here with your effort, happiness arises in the very same moment. This is immediate; who would have to question this any more?

U: Who would have to doubt his own experience?

S: Yes, when happiness has arisen there is no looking for it any more. The answer comes by itself, doesn't it? It doesn't take any time. All of you are bright people, and you have understood the teachings of the wise and compassionate Buddha while still young, even before the words of instruction were complete. Though you understood, at times your mind will think as it pleases, but let us practice. What happens in the mind when we plan to practice to acquire *kusala*? "I'll perform *kusala* later on; now I have to do this quickly." Doesn't this happen to you?

U: It does.

S: Is it good to think and speak like this?

U: No, sir.

S: And then you make efforts and the *viriya-iddhipāda* factor has arisen. What is the right thing to do?

U: The right thing to do is to practice.

S: Yes. If you want to become happier and happier, you have to put forth effort as soon as you have received the instructions of the Buddha and have accepted them. Then the *viriya-iddhipāda* factor will arise. When you make use of this factor that arises in a split second, does it get consumed?

U: It doesn't.

S: Does it diminish?

U: It doesn't.

S: If you decide that the happiness you have is quite sufficient for now and the future and say, "I don't want to progress," can you practice and not progress?

U: One will progress.

S: If you practice not just for a short time, but longer, will you achieve only as much as you get out of a short period of practice?

U: One will get more.

S: This is good, disciple. This is possible because we are now in an auspicious era, because we are born into the right form of existence, and because you make right efforts. The energetic get the true answer even without asking others. Very good. Do you hear? Isn't this so?

U: It is so.

S: So, even if we live with this happiness all the time, it won't diminish; it won't be used up. And what happens if one doesn't want to progress?

U: It isn't possible not to progress, sir.

S: Yes. If you aspire to this there must be many different troubles. Is it possible to attain *bodhi* or not?

U: It is possible.

S: It is possible now and in the future. So let us say, "I don't want to progress," and then focus our minds. Is this possible?

U: It isn't possible not to progress if we work.

S: Do we achieve greater happiness the more we work?

U: We do, sir.

S: We can attain *bodhi* and we can also choose the time and the place of birth. We can then choose a good existence as we wish. When you attain the happiness you desire, what else do you need.

U: Nothing else, sir.

S: You don't need anything; you just have to choose. Is choosing tiresome?

U: It isn't, sir.

S: You can attain it at any time. There are four stages to Nibbāna. Is it possible only for certain types of Ariyas (individuals who have attained one of the four stages)? Do we have to choose the state of Nibbāna?

U: No, sir.

S: What about the place?

U: It isn't necessary.

S: Yes. All by yourself, without any help?

U: It's possible.

S: And in a crowd? If you go outside the pagoda it won't be possible, I think. It is easy, isn't it? The Buddha, the all-compassionate and omniscient, taught many humans, *devas*, and *brahmās* the knowledge that he had attained by penetrating the truth himself. These beings, full of confidence after receiving the teachings, were able to fulfil their aspirations.

As you establish awareness you should establish continuous effort. There are many different types of people. Some are good at reciting or reading or preaching or explaining. I have no doubt about you, disciples, with whomever you compete you will win.

U: Yes, sir.

S: Yes, though others are victorious in their talk, will they achieve anything if they don't practice?

U: No.

S: So, what's the difficulty? Talking is tiresome, isn't it? All we have to do is to make efforts to bring to fruition the aspirations we have made and work as the wise ones of old. Understanding that we have to take up this work our minds will be focused. You are very busy. You may say, "We will practice later when we are free." Does this thought come up still?

U: It does.

S: Sometimes the mind is like that. But I think you don't actually say so?

U: We might, sir.

S: You even speak your mind?

U: We do.

S: Well, if you want to say this, never mind. But for the future can't you burn these impurities out? You have the teachings of the Buddha. When this happens to you, [when you want to procrastinate,] get rid of your doubts. Strive to find the answers without asking others. If you focus right now, won't you get the answers immediately? Isn't this possible?

U: Yes, it is possible, sir.

S: It is possible to focus as you sit here.

U: Yes sir, it is.

S: Is it also possible to maintain the happiness you achieve in this way when you are standing up?

U: It is, sir.

S: Yes. And when you walk?

U: It's possible then, too.

S: Yes, see, it is always possible.

U: If a person is able to maintain awareness, it's possible.

S: What ability do you need? There is nothing difficult in it. Or is it difficult after all?

U: Once a person has acquired proficiency in this, it isn't difficult anymore.

S: He says that it is not possible to simply focus here. Just put your attention here. That's all. Well, isn't that easy?

U: It is easy, sir.

S: It is ever so easy … The Buddha is incomparable. He accumulated virtues without ever resting. He completed his *pāramīs* on his own, working for the welfare of all, didn't he?

U: Yes, he did.

S: And because he could fulfil the *pāramīs* it is easy for us now, isn't it? It is easy. How is it today? You have to raise yourself up happily and complete your work. Then, depending on what your aspirations are, you simply take the bliss you desire. It is very easy. Don't be modest. Don't allow yourselves to think, "This is not possible for me," "This is not suitable for us," "This is not proper for us," "This is not for me." Aim at what you desire. You will get it. Isn't this so?

U: Yes, it is, sir.

S: In the days of the Buddha, too, *devas*, and *brahmās* came to the Buddha, worshipped him, and after they received his teachings, they achieved everything. They completed all their various aspirations, didn't they?

U: They did.

S: Isn't it possible to fulfil your aspiration by establishing unwavering effort while you are a king? Can we count the names of kings who attained complete understanding of the Dhamma?

U: They are without number, sir.

S: Many wealthy people made efforts and attained understanding while continuing their work in business, didn't they?

U: They did.

S: Isn't this possible?

U: It is, sir.

S: Can you count how many wealthy people have done this?

U: No, sir.

S: What about the people who were neither kings nor rich people.

U: They are innumerable.

S: All those who received the teachings and who followed them assiduously fulfilled their wishes, didn't they?

U: They did.

S: Humans and *devas* alike, all of them, lay disciple! What about today, lay disciple? The period is the same, the occasion is the same, the plane of existence is the same. If we simply establish our effort and accept the teachings, do we still have to choose certain times to practice?

U: There is no need for that.

S: Really?

U: That is correct, sir.

S: Yes! The time and the form of existence is right. You can achieve your aspirations when you wish, can't you?

U: That is correct sir.

S: Yes! Do you understand? Before, they didn't practice because they were busy. How is it with this "I'll practice when I'm free"? Do we still have to set times like this?

U: It is not necessary to set aside certain times.

S: What happens if we practice only when we are free? If we stop the practice, then we won't attain what we ought to attain. But now, we do our work and something else as well: we also fulfil our aspirations. We get two things done at the same time, don't we, lay disciples? What is better: to get one thing done or to get two things done at the same time?

U: It is better to get two things done at the same time, sir.

S: You see? It's worth keeping yourself busy. But, even though I say it's worth keeping yourself busy, don't start enjoying being busy just for the sake of being busy—if you want to realize the teachings, I mean. Don't just keep running around all the time. If you establish *viriya* at the same time, the *viriya-iddhipāda* factor will arise. Make yourselves firm in this. If you say that you want to do this work but go on distracting yourselves here and there, your progress will be slow. On the other hand, if you establish this awareness and keep it up, working happily, then you will make progress. What about this work that you can't avoid having to do?

U: We will also make progress with that.

S: Yes, lay disciples. Not only do you get results in this noble work, you get much more besides. What I say is what the Buddha taught. I'm not adding anything.

Now, you are all people making great effort, aren't you? I just wanted to warn you. What I just mentioned [about being too busy] can happen at times.

When you have holidays, you decide to come here and meditate for a few days. Then you have to go back to work and don't get time off anymore. You don't come back. Does this happen sometimes?

U: Yes, it does.

S: Then you abandon the meditation, I think, don't you? Don't abandon it. Carry on with this awareness and at the same time do your work. Then you get two things in one go. You get two. If you postpone the work until your hours of leisure, you get only one benefit. The aspirations you are fulfilling are not ordinary ones, are they? You can attain to the highest, noblest bliss.

Now, what are these aspirations you are going to fulfil? There are the different forms of *bodhi*. *Bodhi* means the penetrative understanding of the Four Noble Truths. If you establish effort, saying that you want to get it, you can fulfil all your various aspirations for *bodhi* right now. This is not ordinary.

How are you going to fulfil your aspirations? Each type of *bodhi* has to be fulfilled in its own way: *sammā-sambodhi* as *sammā-sambodhi*, *pacceka-bodhi* as *pacceka-bodhi*. We must understand it in this way if we are to understand it correctly. It is like planting a mature seed. When it rains, a plant springs up. Here, the plant is nursed well, when you go back home, it has deep roots and is strong.

Is it possible to describe how good this period, this time, is? It is so easy now, lay disciples! Tell me, is this a period when one is oppressed by worries and has to groan and moan?

U: No, sir.

S: Is it a period when we can only stare resignedly?

U: No, sir.

S: It is a period when we can be happy and blissful immediately, when we can never get enough of this joy. You get even more than you wanted. You get even more than you aspired to, don't you, disciple?

U: Yes, sir.

S: Oh yes! You never get tired, not in the present and not in the remainder of *saṃsāra*. What are the teachings of the Buddha? There is nothing in the teachings that causes stress and misery, is there? There isn't! It is pure happiness!

There is one thing, however: the mind may get confused with many thoughts, and I don't think that these thoughts are very pertinent. Now, if you determine to establish this practice, then I don't think that thoughts of doubt will remain at the back of your mind. Can you not be successful in this way? The mind will think what it wills. Let it! Follow the teachings. Do you understand? When you arrive at the goal, you will probably find that it isn't what you expected it to be. Doesn't this happen to people?

U: It has happened many times, sir.

S: Yes, it happens. Dear lay disciples, I am telling you only a little. Those among you who work hard will think, "This monk is reluctant to tell us everything. He is stingy with giving away his knowledge." [Everybody laughs.] You will think, "This is much greater than he said." When you strive for real happiness and in this way arrive at the goal, then you experience something that you cannot describe with all the words there are. Once you've decided, "I'll strive so that I will know for myself," then don't procrastinate. Don't delay. Do you hear? This is so elevated. It is so good, lay disciples. Work hard. Do you understand? You are all people of great effort, aren't you?

U: Almost all of us, sir.

S: Yes. Good, good. Work hard, won't you? You see, when you yourselves arrive at the goal—and for many of you even before that time—you can give this happiness to others. You will never feel reluctant to give. You will want to give a great deal of it, a great deal.

U: This is true, sir. In the course we are conducting now there are three or four students who, after about three days, cry with great sobs because they regret not having come here earlier.

S: Yes, it is like that.

U: They think, "I should have come earlier!"

S: Yes, this happens! Work hard in order to attain the highest. This place is very good.

U: It is a place to which you gave your blessings, Venerable Sayadaw!

S: This is the beginning. I also started from this place.[45] Do you hear me? May this happiness spread slowly out from this place. Yes, yes, you must work hard, strive diligently. Working means that you must meditate at times, and then, at times, you will want to take rest. Does this also happen here?

U: It doesn't, sir.

S: It doesn't?

U: If the students start to meditate at 12.30 P.M., they come out of their meditation cells only at 5.00 P.M. At the beginning, they do take breaks, but after two or three days, they don't come out for breaks anymore.

S: Yes, you see! It's like that! The highest bliss cannot be described in words. But the mind is like a magician. Even though you may be meditating here like this, even though you may be meditating calmly, negative thoughts may arise: "Oh, meditation is so tiring! How can I achieve anything? I can't." Isn't it like that?

U: It is just as you say, sir. They do think that way.

S: Yes. Your mind may be cheating you, but after having established right effort, there is no cheating yourself—or is that still possible?

U: No, sir, it isn't.

S: It is only during the period before you really know that you can cheat yourself.

U: Yes, sir.

S: Even so, you may be saying to yourself that you meditate too long—so take rest now.

Part Two

Further Discourses of Webu Sayadaw

The Power of Forbearance

Webu Sayadaw: At one time Vepacitta, the king of the *asuras*, and Sakka, the king of the Tāvatiṃsa *deva* world, were at war.[1] The *asuras* were defeated and Sakka captured their king, bound him with five ropes around his neck, and confined him in the meeting hall of the *devas*. Of course the king of the *asuras* could not bear this and was overcome with anger. When he saw Sakka enter his royal palace, Vepacitta vilified, defamed, and reviled him from his prison. When Sakka came out of the royal palace again, Vepacitta couldn't refrain from bad-mouthing, slandering, and abusing the king of the *devas*. But Sakka remained calm and serene.

When Sakka's charioteer, Mātali, saw this, he said to Sakka, "Sire, this king of the *asuras* insults you over and over again. Do you accept this so calmly because you are afraid of him?"

Sakka answered, "Young friend, this king of the *asuras* is in my power. I can do with him as I like."

"Then why do you accept this kind of behaviour from him, sire?" Mātali asked.

"He is in my power," Sakka answered. "I can punish him any way I choose, but in spite of this, I forbear with his harangues, defamation, and aspersions."

Why did Sakka act in this way? Because he understood the great benefits that forbearance brings. Though he knew that he could do anything he wanted to his prisoner and that his prisoner would not be able to pay him back, he remained calm and patient. The Buddha said that this is the highest form of patience: to forbear even though you do not have to, even though you could change the situation. Of course it is also good to practice forbearance when you have no other choice, but to forbear voluntarily is the highest and best sort of forbearance.

Sakka has great power, but if he should react to such insults without being the stronger one, what would happen to him?

Disciple: Just like the king of the *asuras*, he would be defeated and have to endure imprisonment. He would have to suffer.

S: Yes, indeed. Whoever tries to be something he is not has to suffer a lot, doesn't he?

So, even though he could have taken action, he observed this practice of developing forbearance in his mind, and that is very noble. The noble ones of old practiced this at all times. Sakka practiced this, as I have just told you, and the Bodhisattas practice this too, don't they?

When our Bodhisatta was reborn as the *nāga* king Bhūridatta, he was very rich.[2] He possessed as many treasures as Sakka.

Having put all his riches aside, he decided to observe the Uposatha precepts. But while he was observing the Uposatha, a snake charmer came along and found the Bodhisatta. Now, compared with the Bodhisatta, he had no power at all. Was our Bodhisatta endowed with power?

D: I don't know this Jātaka story, sir.

S: You know it all right. You are just afraid you'll get tired if you have to tell it.

Now the Bodhisatta's power was so great he could turn someone to ashes by just looking at them sideways. So what use would this snake charmer's spell be against the Bodhisatta? Of no use at all! But the Bodhisatta did not budge because he was afraid of breaking the moral precepts. He did not even open his eyes. So the snake charmer used his tricks on him and brought him under his power. Then he did many things to him. If the Bodhisatta had not wanted to be bothered, he could have flown up into the sky, or dived into the ground, or given the snake charmer a sideways glance. He also could have assumed the appearance of Sakka or a great *brahmā*, couldn't he?

D: He could have, sir.

S: But he didn't do any of these things. So the snake charmer took him by force and put powerful poisons in his mouth. As he did so, our Bodhisatta practiced divine purity of mind and did not react, even to this. Was this because he was weaker than the snake charmer?

D: No. He was strong, but he was forbearing.

S: Why was he forbearing?

D: He was a noble person who had aspired to Buddhahood, and he was fulfilling the perfections (*pāramīs*), sir.

S: If this should happen to you while you are observing the Uposatha, would you act in the same way?

D: I wouldn't be able to endure that, sir. If the person doing it was weaker than me, as in this case, I would flatten him.

S: And if you were someone with great powers?

D: I would certainly use them, sir.

S: Would you remain quiet, not even opening your eyes?

D: Oh no, sir. I would open them very wide.

S: If you act like that, will you get what you want?

D: No, sir.

S: Yes, you see what I mean. The Bodhisatta acted that way. But that was not the end. He was beaten the way washermen beat cloth when they do the laundry, but he didn't react or even move. The Bodhisatta followed the snake charmer's commands for quite some time, remaining calm. He did what the snake charmer told him and even more. And he did all this in order to attain what he aspired to. This is the fulfilling of the perfections. He fulfilled them to the utmost. And did he get results that are inferior to what others get?

D: No, sir. He got results that are higher and nobler.

S: He practiced in order to reach a high level of perfection. Now, if a person is forbearing because he has no choice, that is also good, but if a person doesn't endure when he has to, what will happen?

D: He will suffer, sir.

S: Yes. I have explained a little bit about forbearance now. If I were to explain it fully, there would be no end. Forbearance gives benefits now and for the rest of *saṃsāra*. If you want to be happy in the present, you must work on your patience. If you want to be happy in the future, you must work on your patience. If you want to do something, to accomplish something in your present life, then develop forbearance and patience. Didn't the *nāga* king accomplish this?

D: He did, sir.

S: Yes, he did. The *nāga* king Bhūridatta established himself in and observed morality (*sīla*). If he had simply avoided the difficulty, would he have gained anything?

D: No, sir.

S: If he had escaped into the sky when the snake charmer came, would he have met him and been able to gain perfection in patience and forbearance?

D: No, sir.

S: And if he had assumed the appearance of Sakka?

D: He would not have been able to get results then either, sir.

S: But he didn't use his powers in that way. If he'd just blinked at him, thinking, "This man is bothering me," what would have happened then?

D: The snake charmer would have turned to ashes, sir.

S: But he did none of these things. Even though the snake charmer had absolutely no power over him, he put up with him calmly in order to attain perfection. He didn't even want to budge. He went there to observe the Uposatha and determined that the snake charmer could do with him whatever he wanted. So he endured everything. Once he had made his determination, he carried it through.

How about you? When you undertake the Uposatha observances, when you decide to observe the Uposatha, you keep it, don't you?

D: Yes, sir. We observe the Uposatha.

S: When you take the moral precepts, you observe them for the full day, don't you?

D: We do, sir.

S: After establishing yourselves in the moral precepts, do you keep them, whatever comes your way, no matter what happens?

D: We don't accept everything, sir.

S: But don't you get a full day of practice?

D: No, sir. We don't put in a full day.

S: How much do you get out of one day?

D: After taking the Uposatha precepts, we try to progress for one day, but sometimes we actually regress by more than a day, sir.

S: How much more?

D: Maybe one and a half days, sir.

S: So you take this *sīla* for one day, and then you regress in one day by one and a half days. Is that effort good enough?

D: No, it isn't, sir.

S: Having established ourselves in energy (*viriya*) we can accomplish everything with our patience and forbearance. Is it not possible to apply this everywhere? When you return home from here, you will encounter objects of the senses that you like and objects that you don't like. You constantly encounter these two types of objects. Do you agree that you are confronted with one or the other of these two kinds of objects all the time?

D: There is always either a sense object that we like or one that we don't like, sir. One of the two is always there.

S: When you encounter either kind, forbear! If you live a life of patience and forbearance, what happens when you encounter these sense objects?

D: If we encounter pleasant objects, we reject them through our efforts. And if we encounter unpleasant objects, we establish our efforts more strongly and throw them out.

S: Really? Now, if you meet with pleasant sense impressions, will unskilful states of mind flow in?

D: It is because this might happen, in order to keep them from flowing in that we must establish effort and endure.

S: And if many of these impressions come towards you?

D: Then we have to forbear more, sir.

S: And if you encounter only a few?

D: Then we only need a little forbearance, sir.

S: Now, when you go home and the children talk and make noise—only a little noise, but enough for you to find it intolerable, what do you do?

D: In that case I will have to make an effort to be patient.

S: If you do that, don't you gain?

D: I do, sir.

S: What if they become noisier and more intolerable?

D: Then I will have to make a lot of effort and forbear, sir.

S: Is that so? Will you really do that?

D: I said that in order to give the right answer, sir.

S: You haven't gone home yet, but you have started this practice now. When you practice this you will be strong. It is not tiresome at all. Or do you think you will get tired by living with patience?

D: No, sir, it is not tiresome.

S: Does it cost you anything?

D: It doesn't cost anything, sir.

S: Do you lose anything?

D: Through patience and forbearance we gain much, sir. We don't lose anything. But we are lacking in faith, effort, skill, and wisdom, sir.

S: If you are confused by such thoughts you will think, "Should I do this now? Should I do that?" Then you will be confused. Just remember that you have to be forbearing. Thoughts may come like, "Should I apply this or that? Should I look for this or for that? If this is not there, everything will be in vain." But you should do as we have just said, think only about this one thing.

D: Do you mean that we should just be forbearing, sir?

S: Yes. If you do that, through forbearance everything will go well. Whatever it is, it will be alright.

When I was still a young monk, the Burmese in this country were not very civil, but the Indians were. When I went on my alms round, there was an old Indian man who came running to offer a gift as soon as he saw me. In spite of his old age, this old Indian staggered through the streets selling things, and when he saw me, he came running, even from afar, to give *dāna*.

Now, how is it that our Burmese people were not civil? The parents gave money to the children and they bought sweets and snacks with it. This old Indian was selling what they could afford to buy. Now, how did they call him over? They shouted, "Hey, Indian dog!" They called him that! Did you hear?

So, the children were calling him from every side, and what did he do? He went to them, smiling. He continued to smile, and whoever called to him like that first, he would go to them first. He came to them and they kept calling him "Indian dog." He did not think, "Now, can these boys call me like this to buy something worth a penny—me, an old man who is their senior?" No, he just made the effort to go to those boys.

What would you do if young children called you what they called this old man?

D: We would be angry, of course, sir.

S: Would you just be angry and remain silent?

D: I would not remain silent, sir. Maybe I would even hit those children.

S: Would you get their penny, then? And aside from that what would happen?

D: The Burmese would hit me, sir.

S: Yes, you see, this didn't happen to him. He didn't create any unskilful state of mind, either. He didn't get angry. This is what I encountered when I went on my alms round as a young monk. Even though they called to him like that, he didn't get angry.

If he had been angry, would that have been wholesome (*kusala*) or unwholesome (*akusala*) as an action?

D: Unwholesome, sir.

S: Now, you all want to be forbearing, according to the teachings of the Buddha, don't you?

D: Even though we wish to practice the teachings to some degree, we aren't forbearing to that extent, sir.

S: Don't be distracted by other things. Do just one thing: be forbearing. Do you understand? No matter how much the people living with you upset you, just practice this fully for yourself. What if other people always did the right thing?

D: Then I would be very pleased. But even if they should be chaotic, I should remain calm and pleasant, knowing that if greed arises it will be unwholesome for me, sir.

S: But what will you do if it gets to be too much?

D: I'll be forbearing.

S: Yes. Remember just this. Don't worry about anything else. If you look into this book or that book to see what they say, then your own practice will suffer. Just practice forbearance. If you exert yourself in just this one thing, you can achieve anything.

How Mahā-Kassapa Was Deceived

Sayadaw: There is a king of the Tāvatiṃsa *deva* plane called Sakka, isn't there?

Disciple: Yes, sir.

S: Yes, he is there alright. Sakka, the king of the Tāvatiṃsa world, does exist. Now, how did he become Sakka, the lord of the Tāvatiṃsa *devas*? What merit did he accumulate?

D: He accumulated merit in a former life, sir.[3]

S: It is one thing to accumulate merit in the time when a Buddha's teachings are available, but Sakka's efforts were strong even during the time when the teachings were not there; he depended on his own efforts alone.

He was a wealthy man. He didn't have to worry at all about eating and drinking, and he didn't even have to spend a kyat or half a kyat for a nourishing meal. So he was without any burdens. What did he do? He employed skilled tradesmen and labourers and worked day and night with them without resting. What was he doing? He was working for the welfare of the people. He dug wells and tanks in places where there were none. He built good roads for the travellers and thus spent his life working for the happiness of others. When he worked near his home he stayed at his house, but when his project was in a far off place he worked without even going home. He was happy when others were upright and there were many people working alongside him. Having worked like this without a break, one can face the present and the future. Sakka worked without ever resting until the end of his life span, and because of this he became Sakka.

After the Buddha was awakened and the Triple Gem arose in the world, beings were reborn in the Tāvatiṃsa world at the end of their allotted life span through the force of the merit they attained by revering the Buddha, the Dhamma, and the Saògha. As Sakka is the king of that plane, the other *devas* have to go to show him their respects and venerate him. And what happened? Now these *devas* and *devīs* who had come to the Tāvatiṃsa world as a result of just a small amount of service to the Triple Gem also came to pay respects to Sakka, but their clothes, their bodies, their means of transport and palaces were shining so brightly and splendidly that King Sakka's clothes, body, and palace faded and could hardly be seen in the dazzling light—that's what happened.[4]

Now Sakka's splendid colors and his splendour had not disappeared, but they were outshone by these *devas* and therefore faded. It wasn't apparent any more. It was just like the stars and the moon. When they shine and sparkle at night you look and you can see them. You see them and admire their brightness. But when dawn comes, the sky becomes light. Then the sun comes out, and what happens? Is the light of the stars and the moon still there?

D: The light is still there, sir.

S: Can you see it?

D: The light of the sun outshines them, sir.

S: But can you still see the moon and the stars? Where have they gone?

D: They haven't gone anywhere, sir. They are still there, but because the sunlight is so bright we can't see them, sir.

S: The same was true for Sakka. The *devas* and *devīs* who had been reborn in the Tāvatiṃsa world due to the merit they had gained by showing their respect for the Buddha and his teachings were like the rising sun, and the colors and the glow coming from Sakka faded into obscurity. Now—dear, oh dear!—he was so ashamed he didn't know how to act surrounded by these *devas*. He wished his head would split into many pieces. That's how humiliated he was by all this.

When these *devas* arrived near Sakka's palace, the shine from his clothes, his body, and his surroundings just faded away—so enormous is the difference between merit accumulated within the Sāsana and merit accumulated outside the Sāsana.

Now Sakka was so embarrassed and put out by this that he didn't dare go out any more, and he seems to have remained in hiding.

D: I think Sakka must have been very upset, sir.

S: Wouldn't you be?

D: I would also be very depressed, sir.

S: Even though he was a king, he was in deep trouble. You see, both are good (*kusala*) actions and give merit, but if you apply just a little bit of effort within the Sāsana you get a great deal. That's the difference. But Sakka couldn't change what had happened in the past. Only later did he become powerful again. He understood, "Indeed, the good deeds of charity and other virtuous actions performed within the Sāsana are exceedingly great. They are so much greater than actions performed outside the Sāsana." But even though he understood this, he couldn't do anything about it. He had to continue living as he was.

Once he understood the importance of doing meritorious deeds during the Sāsana, he told the *devas* and *devīs* in his entourage to do good deeds, and they immediately went off to act. They went to where Venerable Mahā-Kassapa lived, and the monk asked them, "Where do you come from?" They replied, "We come from the Tāvatiṃsa world with the intention of performing meritorious deeds, venerable sir."

Mahā-Kassapa, however, said, "Today, I intend to give suffering beings the opportunity to rise above their condition by performing good (*kusala*) deeds. As for you, you are privileged beings. You may return to where you came from." So they had to return to the Tāvatiṃsa world without gaining any merit.

How Mahā-Kassapa Was Deceived

When they reported back to Sakka, he thought to himself, "But I have to get this special merit somehow." Well, he knew that it was good to pay respects to the noble monks when they came out of the cessation state (*nirodha-samāpatti*), so he transformed himself into an old man near Rājagaha—an old man who was very, very poor, without any sons or daughters or grandchildren to look after him. He had to work for a living, even though his body was frail and trembling. He also created a shaky little hut where he lived without any comfort. Sakka's queen, Sujātā, also transformed herself into a decrepit old woman with drooping eyelids and wrinkled skin. And they both lived out in the countryside.

Well, when Mahā-Kassapa saw them, he thought, "These poor old people are poverty stricken and pitiable. They have to work for food and drink, even at the advanced age of eighty or ninety. Today, I'll give these two suffering people an opportunity to rise above their condition." And he stopped at a discreet distance from their hut. Sakka and Sujātā, of course, were only pretending. Still keeping up their deception, they slowly opened their eyes and shielded them with their hands, as if they were trying to see better. Then they approached Mahā-Kassapa.

"Venerable sir," they asked, "are you Venerable Mahā-Kassapa? We are very poor and still have to spend our time working for our daily upkeep. Since you have come, venerable sir, we as disciples will be able to render you a service. Please let us gain merit."

It was necessary for them to deceive him, you see, because if the lie was found out, they wouldn't be able to accomplish what they wanted to do. So they approached Mahā-Kassapa very shyly, very humbly, and then placed celestial food in his bowl. They placed the food in the bowl in the proper manner, and they gave ample portions. As Sakka was offering the food, he said, "Because we venerate generosity and those who receive generous gifts, we offer this with our own hands and with deep respect, sir."

The celestial food, of course, gave off a very pleasant odour. Mahā-Kassapa investigated the matter and realized what Sakka and Sujātā had done. He had not realized before as a matter of course. It was only when he looked into the matter that he knew what had happened. How could he have known before he investigated? Even though he was an Arahat, endowed with great power and supernormal knowledge, he did not know things automatically.

D: Did he not know because he had not concentrated on this matter, sir?

S: When Mahā-Kassapa did not concentrate on a given matter, he did not know about it.

D: That's why he was deceived, sir.

S: But now, Mahā-Kassapa said, "You are Sakka, aren't you?"

"That is correct, sir." Sakka replied. "We did this, sir, because we had to endure so much suffering and distress."

"You are living in a blissful existence with great riches and all sorts of pleasures, aren't you?" Mahā-Kassapa said.

"Yes," Sakka said, "as Sakka I enjoy all these things, sir. I obtained all this power and these pleasures because of the merit I performed when a Buddha-Sāsana was not available. Now that a Buddha has arisen, beings are reborn in the Tāvatiṃsa world as a result of very small deeds they have done. When they come to worship me, they shine so brightly that my own splendour fades away into nothing. Not only that, when they come near my palace, I have to hide, sir."

He had to hide because he was ashamed, you see. He suffered a great deal. He was a powerful king, but he suffered when his subjects came to wait on him. He was powerless to change the situation, and his whole world collapsed. "It would be better if my head split into pieces," he thought. His suffering was that great. That is why he told Mahā-Kassapa, "We are also suffering beings."

Well, once he was successful in performing more merit, he too began to shine. Then poor Sakka could smile and enjoy himself again.

You see, he had accumulated merit in the past, but the merit acquired outside a Buddha-Sāsana and the merit acquired during one are vastly different. I can't stress this enough. So now is the right time; this is a good existence, isn't it?

Dhamma-Asoka's Younger Brother

The emperor Dhamma-Asoka received the Buddha's teachings, and because he was given these instructions and respected and followed them, he could spread them throughout the whole Indian subcontinent.[5] He made sure that the Buddha's religion was foremost, incomparable. His younger brother, the crown prince, however, lived as he pleased. One day, being bored and discontented, he went to the forest for a walk and observed how the deer played and enjoyed themselves in a carefree mood. As he watched them, the following thought arose in him, "These deer enjoy life, happily eating just grass and leaves from the trees, but my brother the emperor donates only the best, most refined food to the monks. The seats he offers them are also the best and the highest. These monks, to whom he gives all these excellent things, whom he venerates and to whom he gives the best living quarters, must also play and enjoy themselves exceedingly well if even the deer, who eat only grass and leaves, have such a good time."

When he went back to the royal palace, he approached the emperor and related his thoughts to him. The emperor thought, "Well, there is no point in explaining this matter to him as he won't understand anyway. Let's wait for a while. Slowly, slowly, I will make him understand." And the emperor remained silent.

Later on, a matter came up with regard to the crown prince which the emperor didn't like at all. He pretended to be angry and had his younger brother called. "You are my younger brother, and as my brother, you will now enjoy the splendour and happiness of an emperor for seven days. When the seven days are up, I shall have you killed." And he issued the appropriate orders. Then he handed his royal power over to the crown prince and repeated that he was going to be on the throne for just seven days and would be killed after that. So the prince was to die in seven days' time.

After this royal order was issued, the crown prince was terribly afraid. He was so afraid he wasn't able to swallow his food. He wasn't able to sleep because he constantly trembled with terror. He kept thinking, "I'll die in seven days."

When the seven days were over, Asoka had his brother called again, and when he saw him, he exclaimed, "Good gracious, you have become thin and haggard and your veins are standing out!" And that was what had happened.

Now the emperor said to his brother, "You are not the same as before. You used to have a handsome appearance. You were strong and good looking. What happened to you now that you have been living in the luxury of an emperor?"

"I was terrified, lord," the prince replied.

"How can this be?" Dhamma-Asoka asked. "You have all the luxuries of the life of an emperor, you should have enjoyed yourself beyond measure, no? What happened?"

"Sire," the prince said, "I wasn't able to enjoy myself at all. Every night I lay awake without being able to sleep for one moment. And what frightened me? I kept thinking that I would have to die without fail when the seven days were up."

So he couldn't enjoy himself. He couldn't even sleep because of the fear of death. His terror was so intense he was unable to enjoy his good fortune in having all the luxuries life can offer. He had only the best of everything. He had the royal insignia and the royal palace, but his fear prevented him from enjoying any of it.

Emperor Asoka said, "Well, little brother, were you as afraid as all that, even though you didn't have to die until seven days were up?"

"That is so, your majesty," the crown prince replied. "I am terrified."

"Well," Asoka said, "you had all the luxuries of an emperor to enjoy, and yet you did nothing but fear your death which was seven days away. The venerable monks live with the knowledge that this mind and body arise and disappear, die and are reborn, billions of times in the wink of an eye. Having understood this, they live in constant dread of these (i.e., mind and matter, *nāma* and *rūpa*). So, did you have to fear your death so much since it was seven days away? The venerable monks who are my masters live as I have just explained. In one instant, as quick as a bolt of lightning striking, mind and matter break up and arise again. There is nothing else for them. Since the monks have experienced this and have seen this for themselves, they are continuously wary of mind and matter."

Now the crown prince understood that the monks could not derive happiness from anything material.

"You were to die after only seven days," the emperor told his young brother, "but my noble teachers go from death to death—they die every moment, not after seven days like you." It was only then that the crown prince understood, and respect for the monks arose in him.

Mahosadha and King Videha

SAYADAW: You all know about the life in which the Bodhisatta was Mahosadha.[6] The Bodhisatta took it upon himself to make all beings happy. Videha, the king, loved the Bodhisatta very much and employed him in his services. Even so, did King Videha recognize the lies of those who were close to him?

DISCIPLE: No, sir, he didn't.

S: Devinda lied to the king, who didn't realize he was lying. He didn't know he was lying because he was lacking in *vijjā* (knowledge). He hadn't worked to acquire understanding in the past when he was developing his *pāramī*, therefore he couldn't even see through the deceptions practiced by other countries. Now, did he understand when those close to him explained things to him?

D: No, sir, he didn't.

S: He couldn't see through the deceptions of others. He really couldn't see through them, and his associates knew that no matter how much they tried to clarify things for him, he wouldn't understand. But a Bodhisatta is concerned with the welfare of all beings. He has a mind that is intent only on making all beings happy, no matter who they are, both now and in the future. He has to make an effort to keep people who lie free from danger, and he makes an effort to protect those who are lied to.

Mahosadha had to accept that the king would not listen to him. Even though the king loved Mahosadha as a son, he listened to other people's lies. Mahosadha didn't like it when the king ignored his advice time after time, but this was due to the king's ignorance. The Bodhisatta had to take care of everything. He had to look after what was happening in the present and what would happen in the future. Only he could take responsibility for the welfare of all beings. He never tired of taking care of others because he did this in order to be perfect in his conduct and in his understanding. Thus he could attain the goal. It was easy for him, but the king couldn't understand.

No matter how much the people around the king explained to him that his adversary had invited him in order to kill him, the king wouldn't believe it. Then the Bodhisatta thought, "By talking to him, trying to make him understand, I am only creating *akusala* for myself. I will make him understand later." So the Bodhisatta pretended to agree with the king and went on ahead of the king. He was happy to do that since in that way he could make sure that there was no danger for the king. He could arrange everything in such a way that the king would eventually see the dangers with his own eyes.

Only when he was already in trouble did the king understand. Devinda did not see through the deception until that moment. When the king was in distress, our Bodhisatta's preparations bore fruit, and everything worked out according to his plans. In this Jātaka, we clearly see who possesses right conduct and right understanding and who doesn't. It is easy to complete both trainings: the training in right conduct (*caraṇa*) and the training in right understanding (*vijjā*).

Don't Destroy Yourselves!

SAYADAW: If we take away even a little bit from the Buddha's teaching rather than preserving it as it is, or, if we add just a few little things, do we further the Sāsana or do we destroy it?

DISCIPLE.: This would destroy the Sāsana, sir.

S: If the teachings are thus altered, do they perish? Or does the person who alters them perish?

D: Only the person who alters them is hurt, sir.

S: Yes, disciples, if the Buddha said, "Practice in this way," then practice only in that way. Don't destroy yourselves.

We have to look after ourselves. We have to look after our sons and daughters, grandsons and granddaughters. It is not possible to just stop looking after ourselves or others. Didn't the Buddha preach that we had to fulfil all our duties towards children and relatives? Where does the fulfilment of these duties belong? It is part of *sīla*, right conduct. Is your *sīla* complete if you don't fulfil your duties?

D: No, sir.

S: Will you be happy if your *sīla* isn't complete?

D: No, sir.

S: Can you fulfil your aspiration for the highest goal if you aren't satisfied with yourselves?

D: It's not possible to make progress in that case, sir.

S: Only if the mind is serene can we attain *samādhi* and only if there is *samādhi* can we really understand. The Buddha preached *samāhito yathābhūtaṃ*. But this you know very well—and not just one aspect of it, but all the different aspects. If we fulfil our duties, in the way we just mentioned, we fulfil *sīla*. We will be happy if we do this. It is easy to attain *samādhi* if we are happy, and *samādhi* is *yathābhūtaṃ*, "as things really are."

You know all this. How do you know this? Through practice. If you know because someone else tells you, you only know words. If you practice, you don't just carry out your duties towards your children and grandchildren, you practice *sīla*. This is *caraṇa-kusala*, the meritorious actions of right conduct. Is it not possible to keep your mind focused, unwavering, below the nostrils, at the spot you touched with your finger just now, while you practice right conduct? If you practice as we mentioned just now, you fulfil right conduct. What do you practice if you keep your mind focused?

D: Understanding, *vijjā*, sir.

S: I think you will say that you have other things to do now, but that later on, when you are free, you will do it. But we have to really face it; we have to accept it just the way the Buddha explained it for us. We will understand that if we do this [fulfil our duties], it will not be in vain. If we neglect to do this, however, our minds will be unsettled. You know enough if you know this. You will be calm. If your mind is calm, you can attain *samādhi*. You may answer that it is easy for monks to do this since they don't have anything else to worry about, but that you are disturbed by your children and grandchildren. Don't you think like that sometimes?

D: We think like that every day, sir.

S: The disciples of the Buddha practiced right action and right understanding simultaneously. This is work. If we don't do this, nothing will come to fruition. If you exert effort, things will fall into place. If you strive with right effort, nothing needs to oppose you.

D: Tell me, sir, if a child cries and we sing it a song and the child smiles again, is singing right conduct in that case?

S: You sing a song because you want to sing. Now, is the child crying because of happiness or because of displeasure?

D: Because of displeasure, sir.

S: His distress is due to your lack of care. If he cries, it's up to you to make him happy. That's all. Does this child cry because he is bad or because he wants to cry or because he is happy or because he hurts?

D: Because he hurts, sir.

S: Does he want his mother or father to help him?

D: Yes, sir, either one of them.

S: So, all you have to do is gently satisfy the child. If you can help the little child in this way, will you be happy or unhappy?

D: If the element of loving kindness (*mettā*) is present we perform a good action, sir.

S: If you are happy, the child's crying will subside. Not only that, the child will start to smile. This is right conduct, disciples. When the child is laughing again, will his mother or father or grandparents still be unhappy?

D: They will be very happy, sir. But, sir, this is *vedayita-sukha*, pleasant sensations, and that is *akusala*.

S: No, it isn't. If you act out of the desire to make the child happy, it is *mettā*. You know much more than I do about all these things that you do in order to make other people happy. You could tell us much more about them. I don't know all that much about it, but even so, I'll tell you a story.

A long time ago, a mother cow in Sri Lanka was separated from her little calf. Do you think that this cow was happy or unhappy about the separation? I think she was very miserable. And what about the calf?

D: He must have been unhappy, too, sir.

S: This cow went in search of her calf. She looked everywhere. The calf was also looking for the mother. Eventually they found each other and immediately they felt deep affection. Before, the little calf had been crying with hunger. The cow had also been crying because of her intense longing for her calf. Do you think that they enjoyed themselves and were happy?

D: This is suffering, sir. And suffering makes us cry.

S: And when they finally found each other, did they smile?

D: Because they had been suffering, they cried, sir.

S: When they found each other, they talked to each other, and only then could the mother give her milk to her hungry calf, her mind full of love. This is *mettā*, disciples—*mettā* that is one-pointed. There was no other thought in her mind aside from her love for her calf. At that moment a hunter threw a spear at her. Does it say in the story that the spear pierced her?

D: It didn't pierce her, sir.

S: It didn't pierce her. That's right. Do you hear? Do you think the cow knew about these advantages, these benefits, that come through *mettā*?

D: She didn't know about them, sir.

S: Was she unable to develop loving kindness because she didn't know these things?

D: She was practicing loving kindness, sir.

S: Because she had this *mettā*, she couldn't be killed by this spear. If you throw a spear, you throw it to kill, and this hunter had a very sharp spear. As this cow was full of loving kindness, it seems she only felt as thought a little palm leaf had pricked her. If you throw a palm leaf at a cow, does it penetrate deeply into the flesh? What happens?

D: The palm leaf will bounce off the cow, sir.

S: Yes, you see? It is said that this spear bounced off just like it was a palm leaf. You all know about the advantages and benefits of a mind full of loving kindness. You can explain all this.

D: But we can't, sir.

S: Of course you can. Why? Because the Noble Ones who are the masters of loving kindness and compassion have explained the benefits of *mettā* to you, both in detail and in brief. You have all become proficient in this. But let's not talk about spears and things like that. Let's just take the example of a tiny mosquito that pricks you with its little stinger. Will it penetrate your skin or not?

D: As far as I'm concerned, sir, it will.

S: You'll send it *mettā*, won't you?

D: Giving *mettā* is something I do only with my mouth, sir.

S: So, what happens when a little mosquito stings you?

D: I don't really want to talk about this, sir. It's a little embarrassing to have to answer this in front of everyone else, sir. I usually hit the mosquito and brush it off.

S: But you do practice non-hatred, don't you?

D: My non-hatred is not very perfect, sir. I just hit it.

S: This is called sending *mettā*, isn't it? Is it difficult to practice *mettā*? To remember *mettā*?

D: For us, sir, it is fairly difficult.

S: Wait. I'll ask you another question. What would you say? Which is higher, a man or a cow?

D: Human beings are much higher than cows, sir.

S: Really? What about *pāramī*? Would you say that a man has more *pāramī* than a cow?

D: We became human beings because of our *pāramī*, sir.

S: The poor cow doesn't understand anything. But you send *mettā*, reciting *sabbe sattā averā hontu* ("May all beings be free of enmity"). The cow just experienced *mettā* for her little calf, and that is why the spear did not penetrate her. You understand this clearly, profoundly, and you can explain it to others.

D: We can't, sir.

S. Yes, yes, you are able to explain this. Now, among lower forms of life such as bovines, which are not endowed with *pāramī*, which is higher, the males or the females?

D: They are both the same, sir.

S: If we had to decide which of these is more powerful, which would you choose?

D: The bull is more powerful, sir.

S: So—they are not the same?

D: The bull is the leader, sir. The cow can't lead.

S: We have just been talking about a mere cow, haven't we? And yet, this [higher power of *mettā*] was possible for her.

D: She could do this because she was a mother. We have never collected our minds to that extent in *mettā*, sir.

S: If I should say that the cow is therefore happier than man, what would you reply?

D: In this example, the cow has a very clear mind, sir.

S: Do you accept this? Do you accept what this disciple said? "We're not as developed as this cow"? You others—you may not want to accept this.

D: I alone am responsible for what has been said, sir. I don't know. Maybe they will beat me up when I leave this assembly. These are just my personal views.

S: So, who is happier?

D: We'll have to leave it like that, sir.

S: So, if I say, "This disciple doesn't even have as much understanding as a cow," are you happy with that?

D: I don't like it, sir, but since it's the truth, I'll have to accept it.

S. What if I call you "The disciple who is equal to a cow"?

D: That's a bit better, sir, as in this case at least I'm on the same level with a cow.

S: The cow wasn't pierced by the spear because of her loving kindness. How about you? Would the lance enter your body?

D: It probably would, sir.

S: Then can we say that you are equal to the cow? It is true. You all have *pāramī*. What are you deficient in, then? You need effort (*viriya*). Do you hear? What is effort? It means to determine: "Hey, I'll work!" With this attitude, nothing is difficult. Yes, what you need is effort, determination. You know that, of course. Will you find things difficult if you make the following determination: "I'll establish effort that is equal to the effort put forth by the disciples of the Buddha"? Even a cow could do it. The Buddha's teachings are there, but the cow didn't need to know them. There was no knowledge of the Buddha's teachings in the cow. Tell me, was she born in a good plane of existence?

D: She wasn't, sir.

S: Her mind was one-pointed through *mettā*. If we practice in the same way, won't we become even more tranquil than this cow? If we reach the necessary calm and are able to maintain it, won't we be able to practice right action? Once purity of action is established, we can proceed to concentrate on the touch sensation of the breath at the nostrils. Can't we attain understanding in this way and proceed to fulfil our aspiration for awakening.

Going Home

A Discourse at the IMC-Yangon [Extract]

Webu Sayadaw: Now that you have exerted much effort on meditation, you have had some positive achievement. Now, when you go home, do you have to give this to your wife?

Answer: No, sir, I do not have to give it. But she would scowl at me and say I have done this only for my own good and that I was selfish.

S: Well then, from here you have experienced the beneficial effects of the Dhamma, and when you meet your wife and children at home I think you have failed to mention how the practice of the Dhamma has produced positive results in you.

A: I did not get a chance to explain at all, sir. The moment I reached home she greeted me with a scowl.

S: Well, now after you have taken the precepts (*sīla*) what did I say? I said that now that you have taken *sīla* you must observe and practice this *sīla* to the fullest extent. This is in accordance with the Buddha's teachings. If you practice in this manner, all your wishes will be fulfilled in this lifetime as well as in the future. That was how I reminded you. In practicing *sīla* you must perform all those acts required of a layman. A person who has a sound and complete *sīla* is indeed a wholesome person. In the case of the Saògha, the Buddha also laid down the relevant rules of conduct. Only when you practice and observe *sīla* to the fullest extent can it be said that your *sīla* is complete.

Now when you go home, if you have experienced joy that arises from the full observance of *sīla*, you would have *mettā* for your wife at home and you would, accordingly, have greeted her with such feelings. But since you did not greet her so, she scowled at you. That is why when you return from here this time, you must greet her, talk to her, and treat her in a manner which will be agreeable to her and in accordance with *sīla*. Even before reaching your house you should have *mettā* for her and the wish that she may also enjoy the peace that you yourself have achieved. When you reach home it should be you who greets her pleasantly and with *mettā*.

A: Sir, when I returned home from here, my mind was so occupied with thoughts about *nāma* and *rūpa* (mind and matter) that I failed to smile at her.

S: Well, *nāma-rūpa* is of course *nāma-rūpa*. But since you did not greet her with a smile as you did before, she scowled at you. What you should have done was to greet her in the way I explained just now. This is also *sīla*. She should also have the peace that you have had. Now, although you have greeted her suitably and she is still not pleased, in such a case, who is still lacking in *sīla*? Here you must regard yourself as still lacking in the fulfilment of your *sīla*. You should then remember that you must make her happy and that you are still wanting in *sīla*. So you greet her again or call her again agreeably.

Now, when you first greet her, if you wish that she should also enjoy the fruits of Dhamma that you have experienced and if you have *mettā* for her, merit has already accrued to you for that action. So you are, in a way, the gainer. If your greeting meets with success, so much the better. But suppose it does not meet with success and you have to try again. In that case, have you lost or gained anything by your first actions? You know you have lost nothing. In fact, by having to try again you will be gaining more merit, and so you should be happy for it.

So you must try again and again, making changes in yourself until you succeed. But the change must come from you. Don't be angry; don't be short-tempered if there is no success. You must regard yourself as still wanting in this respect.

Now suppose I tell you that there is a big water pot that is used by many and that you should fill this pot with water. You know that the more water there is in the pot, the greater will be the number of people who can use it. So you will no doubt fill it to the brim. So it will not be necessary for me to tell you whether it is full or not. You will know yourself. So you see, if your wife smiles when you greet her, then you will know that the water pot is full.

Words of Wisdom

Always Spoken by Ven. Webu Sayadaw[7]

After you have taken the vow of *sīla* (morality), fulfil it. Once you have fulfilled it, all your wishes will be fulfilled. It will bring happiness to you now and also in the future.

There is nothing besides the words of the Buddha that will bring peace and happiness to one in the present existence as well as in one's future lives in *saṃsāra*. The words of the Buddha are embodied in the Tipiṭaka, the three baskets of knowledge. The Tipiṭaka is voluminous, so we must take the essence of it. The essence of the Tipiṭaka is the thirty-seven factors of awakening (*bodhi-pakkhiya-dhamma*). The essence of the *bodhi-pakkhiya-dhammā* is the Noble Eightfold Path. The essence of the Noble Eightfold Path is the three *sikkhās* (trainings), and the essence of the three *sikkhās* is *eko dhammo* or the "one and only Dhamma."

The three *sikkhās* are: *adhisīla* (higher morality), *adhicitta* (higher mentality), and *adhipaññā* (higher wisdom).

When one is mindful of *nāma* and *rūpa* (mind and matter), there will be no physical and mental violence. This is called *adhisīla* (higher morality).

When *adhisīla* develops, the mind becomes concentrated and tranquil. This is called *adhicitta* (higher mentality, higher concentration).

When *adhicitta* (*samādhi*) develops, one gains insight into the real nature of *nāma-rūpa*. In a flash of lightning, *nāma-rūpa* undergoes incessant change billions of times. This ever-changing process is beyond the control of any *deva* or *brahmā*. One who knows by insight the process of becoming and cessation achieves *adhipaññā* (higher wisdom).

The most obvious thing to one and all is the breathing process. The nose is a prominent part of the body. The out-breath and the in-breath are always touching the nostrils.

The nostrils are the sensitive part of the nose which the out-breaths and the in-breaths touch as they come out or go in. In other words, the wind element or element of motion comes into contact with the nostrils, producing a sensation. Both the wind element and the nostrils are *rūpa*, and it is *nāma* that knows the contact or sensation. Ask no one what *rūpa* and *nāma* are. Be mindful of the nostrils. One knows the sensation of breathing in. One knows the sensation of breathing out. Keep on knowing the in-breath and the out-breath and there will be no chance for greed, hatred, and delusion (*lobha*, *dosa*, and *moha*) to arise. The fires of greed, hatred, and delusion are extinguished and the result is calm and peace of mind.

One cannot know the sensation before contact is made. One can no longer know the sensation when the contact has disappeared. One must take notice of the actual contact. This is called the immediate present.

Be mindful of the present continuously. If you can keep on knowing the present for twenty-four hours at a stretch, the good results will be evident. If you cannot be mindful of what is taking place at every moment continuously, you will fail to notice what happens in a flash of lightning and find yourself on the debit side.

If you are mindful of the contact of the breath on the nostrils, you will realize that there is only *nāma* and *rūpa*. Besides *nāma* and *rūpa*, there is no such thing as I, he, or you; there is no self, no man, no woman. You will know for yourself that the Buddha's teaching is the truth, only the truth, nothing but the truth. You will not need to ask anyone about it. Awareness of the contact between the wind element and the tip of the nose produces there and then the knowledge that there is no such thing as *attā*: self or soul.

At these moments of awareness, one's comprehension or insight (*ñāṇa*) is clear. That is called *sammā-diṭṭhi*: right understanding or right view. There is nothing else besides *nāma* and *rūpa*. This is called analytical knowledge of mind and body (*nāma-rūpa-pariccheda-ñāṇa*).

The continuous practice of this contemplation eliminates the notion of *attā* or self, and produces a clear vision or knowledge. This benefit is the result of momentary contemplation. Do not think it is not much. Do not think that nothing is known, that no benefit accrues during meditation. Such benefits can be gained only during the Buddha Sāsana. While meditating, forget about food and other necessities. Strive with diligence for progress in gaining the insight that will end in the realization of knowledge of the path (*magga-ñāṇa*), knowledge of the fruition state (*phala-ñāṇa*), and Nibbāna.

The Path To Be Followed[8]

1. The teachings of the Buddha contained in the Tipiṭaka have but one object: liberation from suffering. Methods vary but the objective is the same. It is not necessary to follow all the methods. Choose one of them, and then put it into practice with adequate energy and in a steadfast manner.

2. *Vijjā* (knowledge) and *caraṇa* (conduct) must be developed simultaneously. Two things can be done at the same time.

3. Follow the teaching of the Buddha as well as that of the teacher. Be respectful. Be humble. *Khanti* (patience) and *mettā* (loving kindness) must be practiced assiduously.

4. *Vipassanā* means to see what really is. Meditators must see things as they really are, otherwise it is not *vipassanā*.

5. What really is, is not to be sought elsewhere; it is in one's own body. It is ever present there. It is unavoidable. It is *nāma-rūpa* (mind-matter).

6. Of all the manifestations of *nāma* and *rūpa* in the body, the in-breath and out-breath are not easily recognizable but they are easy to contemplate.

7. The process of breathing in and out begins with birth and ends only with death. It goes on without any pause or break. It is always there, whether one is working, talking, studying, or sleeping.

8. Although the process of breathing in and out is continuous, it is hardly noticed by unmindful people. As the Burmese saying goes, "Those who are unmindful would not notice a cave. Those who are mindful would notice even the mist." Only those who are mindful will be aware of the breathing process.

9. Here, awareness means that the meditator takes note of the in-breath as it touches the nostrils and of the out-breath as it touches the nostrils. As breathing is continuous, so awareness must be continuous too. Only then can awareness be properly called *vipassanā* meditation.

10. There are twenty-four hours in a day. If your awareness can be continuous for twenty-four hours, the beneficial results will be very clear. If possible, the ascetic practice of always sitting (*nesajjika-dhutaòga*) should be performed. What the Buddha teaches is not suffering but the cessation of suffering. In the Buddha's lifetime, those who performed this ascetic practice of always sitting were healthier and lived longer. If you give in to sleepiness and go to sleep, you are likely to sleep forever in the round of rebirths (*saṃsāra*). If you wish to sleep, go to that place where no sleep is necessary.

11. Being mindful of what really is, or seeing things as they really are, that is the main purpose of the three *sikkhās*, the Noble Eightfold Path, the thirty-seven *bodhipakkhiyas*, in short, of the entire Tipiṭaka. They are all covered, as it were, in one stroke.

12. Touch or contact is *rūpa*. Knowing or awareness is *nāma*.

13. Appearance and disappearance of vibrating manifestations are the process of becoming and cessation.

14. As meditators notice the swiftly changing process of appearance and disappearance of contact sensations at the nostrils, concentrated insight (*vipassanā-samādhi*) develops in due course, that is to say, after a considerable length of time. The concentration developed in this way becomes more and more intense until a meditator becomes aware of swiftly sweeping changes all over the body.

15. When these swiftly sweeping changes are seen with insight, the characteristic of *anicca* becomes most obvious, and accordingly the characteristics of *dukkha* and *anattā* are also seen. It is not necessary to utter them by word of mouth. *Vipassanā* meditation means being mindful of what actually happens. Mindfulness develops day by day, and consequently, meditators gain penetrating insight.

16. As meditators develop concentration, their insight develops as well, culminating in the realization of path knowledge (*magga-ñāṇa*) and fruition knowledge (*phala-ñāṇa*). This realization is as evident and satisfying as quenching your thirst by drinking water. The meditator who has realized the path and fruition has realized it by himself in this present lifetime, not hereafter. Therefore, the result of his practice is "seen by himself and in self" (*sandiṭṭhiko*).

17. After the knowledge of the path and the fruition is attained, if someone wishes to regain the attainment of the fruition (*phala-samāpatti*), he has to return to the practice of *vipassanā* and progressive realization. The attainment of the fruition (*phala-samāpatti*) can be compared to one's own dwelling.

18. With firm faith and unflagging energy, be mindful of the contact of the breath with the nostrils without any letup or break. Do not waver. Do not procrastinate. Do it now, and the sustained practice will yield results forthwith. The result is the end of being tormented by passions and the enjoyment of indescribable bliss. Therefore, the results of the practice are immediate (*akāliko*).

How to Fulfil Sīla

Do meritorious deeds such as cleaning a pagoda or watering the Bodhi tree, or by serving your teacher or parents, or even by attending to the needs of your family—all these will go into the credit side of your fulfilment of *sīla*. While doing these things, you can still meditate. If you neglect any of these duties, can you say for certain that you have fulfilled *sīla*? If *sīla* is unfulfilled, can you acquire the happiness you are looking for? If there is no happiness, no peace, you cannot get *samādhi*. Without *samādhi* you cannot acquire *paññā*.

Practicing a Brief Teaching

A Discourse to Western Students[9]

Sayagyi U Chit Tin: These are the disciples of Sayagyi U Ba Khin—fifteen foreign disciples, men and women. Today is the fifth anniversary of Sayagyi U Ba Khin's death. Fifty monks were offered breakfast very early this morning, and about 150 disciples were invited to the feeding ceremony. These disciples have been coming for the whole month for their *vipassanā* courses at the Centre. These people can stay in Burma for only seven days. So they do meditation for seven days, leave for Bangkok or Calcutta, then come back here again. Some of them are on their second trip. More will be coming for a third trip. The meditation course is arranged for the whole of this month to commemorate the passing away of Sayagyi. Some of the students are from America, some from England, France, and New Zealand—very far away places, representing many nationalities. Some have come from Australia, and there is one disciple from Malaysia.

Webu Sayadaw: This is just like the time of our Lord Buddha. Then also they arrived in the presence of the Buddha all at the same time. Not from the same country, not from the same town, the same place, but from different countries, different towns—all men of noble hearts, arriving simultaneously at the same place to pay respects to the Lord Buddha. Noble beings, whether human or celestial, never tired in giving homage to the Lord Buddha. Glad in their heart, they worshipped the Buddha in great adoration. The Buddha, having unbounded love, pity, and compassion for all beings, showed them the way. They followed and practiced his teachings with meekness and in all humility, being good and disciplined students. Wandering forlornly throughout the whole of *saṃsāra* (continued rebirths), looking for a way out, they have now reached the end of their journey. They have now found what they have been searching for during the whole of *saṃsāra*. Innumerable were those who attained Nibbāna by following the Buddha's advice.

Now you are all just like those seekers of the old days. And just like them, if you are determined to acquire what they did and if you are equipped with noble zeal and earnestness, having now reached a place of sanctity, where the Buddha's teachings are kept alive, doing all that it is necessary to do, following the teachings with meekness and humility, without wasting time, working hard in this way—being able to work hard in this way, you will achieve what you have been working for: the supreme goal of the holy life. This is something you should all feel happy about.

Do they understand what I have said? I wonder if they do.

SAYAGYI U CHIT TIN: One or two might understand, sir. They have learned some Burmese in America.

WEBU SAYADAW: Have they? Well, very good. I am glad. The ones who understand can then pass on the teachings of the Buddha to the others, thus benefiting many. Isn't that so? Who is the one who can speak Burmese fluently? So, disciple, you understand Burmese. Do you understand me? Only a little? Well, a little will be useful. Understanding only a little of what the Buddha taught will be of great help. Just a few of the Buddha's words are not really a little. They mean a great deal. There is something that you have longed for and worked for throughout *saṃsāra*. When you understand the teachings of the Buddha and follow his advice, you will achieve what you have been looking for.

Now, what is it you wish to gain, for now and for always, throughout endless *saṃsāra*? What do I mean by now? I mean the immediate present. Right this moment. You all want happiness, relief from suffering right now. Don't all of you want that? And you all want to be assured of happiness in *saṃsāra*, too. Well, during all your rebirths in *saṃsāra* you are all the time subjected to old age, illness, and death. It means great suffering. You are all afraid of old age, illness, and death, aren't you? Yes, you all are, I'm sure. Being frightened, you don't want to have anything to do with them, do you? What you really long for is a place where these sufferings don't exist—a place of happiness where these things are absent, where old age, illness, and death are unknown, where all these sufferings cease—in short, Nibbāna. This is what you are striving for. If you will follow the Buddha's instructions with all meekness and due humility, you will achieve your goal, won't you? You will have accomplished all your work, having gained success, having gained what you have always longed for.

So, what you understand may be very little: only a short brief teaching. But if you follow it diligently, the achievement will not be small. It is what you have been striving for throughout the ages. Can that be regarded as only a small reward? Not at all. It is indeed a big reward. Once you understand the instruction, however brief and concise, and follow it carefully, without ceasing, happiness will be yours. There will be happiness for all the universe, for all humans, *devas*, and *brahmās*. Although the teaching may be only a few words, the achievement will be great. All you want is achieved. Is that not so? Indeed it is.

So, disciple, can you manage to follow and practice that short instruction? Can you? Very good. Like you all, at the time of the Blessed One, there were people who wandered forth, looking for peace and happiness for all time. They were looking for it before the Awakened One had made his appearance yet. Who were they? Oh, you can say the whole world. But I will single out for you the example of Sāriputta and Moggallāna, the auspicious pair, who later became the two chief disciples of the Blessed One.[10]

Maybe you are acquainted with the story of their going forth. Sāriputta and Moggallāna were living the holy life as wanderers, looking for the Deathless. It was Sāriputta who first came into contact with one of the five disciples who had learned the Doctrine from the Blessed One. The wanderer Sāriputta saw him going around for food. Seeing his faculties serene, the color of his skin clear and bright, Sāriputta at once knew that he possessed the knowledge of the way he had been looking for. Sāriputta followed the holy monk until he had finished his round and left the town with his alms food. The wanderer Sāriputta waited at a respectful distance while the holy monk ate his meal. Then, Sāriputta went up to him, paid courteous respects, and asked him about his Teacher and the Doctrine he taught.

All this is in the Piṭakas (Canon),but I will give you just a short summary. The holy monk replied that he had gone forth under the Blessed One, who was his Teacher, and that it was the Blessed One's Doctrine that he followed. When Sāriputta pressed for an exposition of the Doctrine, the holy monk said, "I have only recently gone forth. I have only just come to this Doctrine and Discipline. I cannot teach you the Doctrine in detail. I can only tell you its meaning in brief."

This holy monk had actually reached the supreme goal, so he must have known the whole Doctrine, but out of humility, he confessed that he knew only a little. Then Sāriputta, who later became the chief exponent of the Blessed One's Doctrine, said that he did not want much. He only wanted to hear a little of what the Buddha taught. The holy monk granted his request. He gave him only a sketch of the Doctrine. How little was it? So little it was not even a whole stanza. When Sāriputta heard the short statement of the Doctrine, he said that it was sufficient for him. For the spotless, immaculate vision of the whole Dhamma had arisen in him after hearing just a little of it.

So the teaching was only a few words, but Sāriputta's understanding was not little at all. He understood the whole Doctrine. So, disciple, you too understand a little, don't you? Well, if you do, and follow the Blessed One's advice, your achievement will be very great.

I, of course, cannot speak your language. So you, disciple, if you understand a little, pass it on to your friends so all of you will know a little of the Dhamma. Can't you do this? I'm sure you can.

All of you have created, each one of you, great *pāramīs*. That's why you are all here, coming from various countries, distant lands, far, far away from here. But because you have acquired sufficient *pāramīs* you all arrive here at the same time, simultaneously from different countries. And having reached here, you want to know the Doctrine. So you have heard the Doctrine.

You have learned the Buddha's advice. But you do not remain satisfied with just hearing the Doctrine and just remembering it. You want to practice it. So you strive energetically and begin to walk the path. You establish the necessary effort (*viriya*), and in time, you must surely enjoy the fruits of your effort. Even now you know, of course, don't you? You're getting results commensurate with your application and diligence.

You are all here now because you have acquired sufficient *pāramīs* to do so. The Blessed One said that if you stay with the Dhamma and follow the Doctrine you are dwelling near him although physically you may be at the other end of the universe. On the other hand, if you reside near him, so near, so close that you could hold the ends of his robes with your hands, yet, if you don't follow his advice and practice the Doctrine according to his instructions, there is the whole distance of the universe between him and you. So, you live in various countries—far, far away. And yet, you are all so close to the Blessed One. Following his advice diligently, with due meekness, you will achieve what you wish, you will win the goal that you have strived for throughout *saṃsāra*. Innumerable are the holy ones who have trodden the path and reached Nibbāna. So also, you, from different countries, different towns, all holy people, arriving simultaneously at the place of sanctity, if you set up sufficient effort (*viriya*) and work diligently with all humility you will also arrive at your goal.

This is really an occasion for happiness and joy. We all can't help being buoyant in spirit, cheering and admiring you, seeing your wonderful devotion and zeal. I wish you all success. Well done! Well done!

Part Three

Webu Sayadaw and Sayagyi U Ba Khin

Venerable Webu Sayadaw and Sayagyi U Ba Khin were closely linked in their Dhamma work beginning with their first meeting in 1941. Webu Sayadaw urged Sayagyi U Ba Khin in unmistakable terms to teach meditation and effectively gave him his mission to spread the Dhamma. He continued to encourage and support him throughout his life in various ways. In 1953, Sayagyi U Ba Khin invited the Sayadaw to visit his newly established meditation centre in Inya Myaing Road in Yangon (Rangoon). People who knew the Sayadaw did not think he would accept the invitation as he had never made visits outside his three meditation centres in Upper Myanmar (Burma), but to everyone's surprise he immediately accepted the invitation conveyed to him by one of Sayagyi's disciples.

Ven. Webu Sayadaw undertook his first journey to Lower Myanmar in response to Sayagyi's invitation and spent seven days at the International Meditation Centre. Afterwards, he visited Lower Myanmar every year, including Sayagyi's Centre, to give talks and teach. Seven years later, in 1960, he was at the Centre again from May 12th to May 17th.

Sayagyi used to consult Webu Sayadaw on matters connected with his teaching, and when he wrote a treatise in Burmese entitled The Basic Study of the Buddha's Teachings and Their Correct Application, he submitted it to Webu Sayadaw for approval in 1953.[5] In his introduction to the book, Sayagyi wrote, "What we have found and what I am describing here are merely our findings and our analysis. I do not consider everything presented here to be completely, absolutely proven. If there are mistakes, I request that others correct me. I would like to invite pertinent criticism as well as comments from those who have a mature knowledge of the texts (*pariyatti*) and from those Noble Ones who follow the Teachings—those who have practiced extensively in the past and who continue to practice diligently today. It is my aim to do further work based on such comments—to either answer and clarify them or accept them."

In mentioning "those Noble Ones who follow the Teachings—those who have practiced extensively in the past and who continue to practice diligently today." Sayagyi was especially thinking of Ven. Webu Sayadaw. He told the Sayadaw, "This booklet was written in accordance with the instruction I received from you. This is how I have been teaching *vipassanā*, based on first-hand experience. This is the way I discovered the common factors involved in extraordinary achievements."

Before publishing the text, Sayagyi sent a copy to Ven. Webu Sayadaw for his comments. Webu Sayadaw approved the text of The Basic Study in a handwritten letter, saying, "I received Sayagyi U Ba Khin's text through my lay disciple Maung Bo. From the day U Ba Khin received the Teachings of the Buddha, he has practiced and fulfilled them without interruption. Now he has reached the position of Accountant General and at the same time he is striving to benefit others through the Buddha's Teachings. He has understood perfectly what only Noble Ones can understand—those Noble Ones who truly follow and fulfil the Buddha's Teachings, who practice the three trainings (*sikkhā*) of *sīla*, *samādhi*, and *paññā* in all their pristine purity in accordance with the Pāḷi scriptures. He has made lofty aspirations, and the treatise he has submitted is impressive. I believe that this booklet will spread the fragrance and the light of the Sāsana as it is in agreement with the aims of true Buddhists. You have given a great deal [in this book]. Now be mindful."[6]

In 1965, Sayagyi U Ba Khin ordained for ten days under Webu Sayadaw in his forest monastery and meditation centre at Ingyinbin, Webu Sayadaw's birthplace.

The following sections give relevant extracts from the biography of Sayagyi U Ba Khin written by his disciple U Ko Lay, former vice-chancellor of the University of Mandalay, with additional material contributed by Sayagyi U Chit Tin.

From Yangon to Webu

In 1941, Sayagyi became the Accounts Officer for Burma Railways. That year, the fire of war was ablaze in the world; the skies of Myanmar were also overcast with the clouds of war. In July, Sayagyi took an express train, using his special carriage, to inspect the accounts in Myit Tha railway station. When he found that another railway accounts officer had already done so, he had some free time. His carriage was pulled to Kyauksai station where it was shunted aside as he had a few days' work to catch up on. Due east from the railway station, there was the dark silhouette of Shwe Tha Lyaung Hill, which seemed to beckon Sayagyi. He went there without delay accompanied by the assistant station master of Kyauksai to pay respects at the pagoda on the hill. After doing so, he looked around, enjoying the lush verdant landscape.

In the north there was a small hill, and at its foot they could see a small bamboo-hut monastery. When Sayagyi asked his companion about it, he replied that a monk worthy of veneration was living in the hut, and since he had chosen to live at the foot of Webu Hill, they called him Webu Sayadaw. The people who lived nearby venerated and respected this Sayadaw as they believed he was an Arahat. Sayagyi instantly felt a thrill inside him and wanted to go and pay respects to this Sayadaw. He started to descend directly towards the little hill, but his escort told him that it was not possible to descend from that side of the mountain. "The Sayadaw doesn't receive visitors now," the assistant station master added. "I'll accompany you to his place in the afternoon."

Back at the station, they had lunch. Then Sayagyi went to meditate in his carriage. He concentrated with *mettā* on Webu Sayadaw and informed him in his mind that he wanted to come and pay respects. At three o'clock in the afternoon, Sayagyi called his companion and they took a horse carriage to Webu Valley. When the road became too rough, they descended and continued on foot. As they entered Webu valley, their minds became very quiet and serene. They saw the Konawin Pagoda, which is nine cubits high, and the Sīmā Hall[7] and paid their respects.

The little door of the hut suddenly opened and Webu Sayadaw's face appeared. "What wish do you have in mind as you pay respects, great lay disciple?" were the Sayadaw's first words.

"Oh, you want Nibbāna," the Sayadaw said. "How will you go there?"

"Sir, the way to Nibbāna is the knowledge gained through *vipassanā*, *paññā*," Sayagyi replied. "I am also directing my mind to the awareness of *anicca* at this moment."

"Oh," the Sayadaw said, "*sādhu*, *sādhu*, *sādhu* (well done). How did you receive this Dhamma?"

Sayagyi replied that he had meditated for seven days under the guidance of his teacher and benefactor Saya Thet Gyi; then he had continued on his own. Even when travelling, as he was at that time, he meditated in his railway carriage.

"Then you have *pāramī*, great lay disciple," the Sayadaw said. "I thought that you must have spent a long time by yourself in the forest and that you must have made great efforts there."

They spent more than one hour conversing in this way, then after having obtained permission to offer a vegetarian meal early the next morning, Sayagyi and the assistant station master returned to Kyauksai station. The next day they cooked the meal and went to offer it to Webu Sayadaw. He accepted the food and gladdened them again with talk on the Dhamma. The other people who came to offer breakfast said that Webu Sayadaw had never talked that much before. At the end, he said, "Great disciple, you have to give the Dhamma, share the Dhamma you have with everyone. You cannot be sure that you will meet again the disciples who are here with you now. Now that you have met them, give them the Dhamma. Show them the Dhamma to some small extent.

Give the Dhamma. Do not wait." In this way, Webu Sayadaw admonished and stirred Sayagyi.

Sayagyi heeded the Sayadaw's words. Back at the station in Kyauksai, he taught the assistant station master in his railway carriage. That man was the first person to be taught the Dhamma by Sayagyi U Ba Khin.

Sayagyi's Invitation to Webu Sayadaw[8]

In 1953, Sayagyi sent U Boon Shein, who worked in the Accountant General's Office, to Kyauksai to make a formal invitation to Ven. Webu Sayadaw. Sayagyi did not give U Boon Shein a formal letter of invitation for the Sayadaw. "Just say that I sent you," Sayagyi said and gave him instructions concerning the invitation. He added that he would also invite the Sayadaw from Yangon.

U Boon Shein's first stop was at a friend's house in Mandalay. "So, it's the great U Boon Shein," his friend said in greeting him. "What brings you to Upper Myanmar so unexpectedly?"

"My teacher has sent me here on a special mission," U Boon Shein replied. "I came on the first available plane. Can you get me a car, my friend?"

"Who is your teacher? And just what is your special mission?" his friend asked.

"My teacher is Sayagyi U Ba Khin, the Accountant General," U Boon Shein replied. "A group of us in the Accountant General's Office have set up a Vipassanā Association and opened a meditation centre. We've built a pagoda there. The Accountant General is the teacher at the centre; that's why we call him 'Sayagyi' (revered teacher). He has asked me to invite Ven. Webu Sayadaw to come to Yangon, so I have to go to Kyauksai."

"You must be mad, U Boon Shein," his friend said. "Ven. Webu Sayadaw doesn't even come to Mandalay. What makes you think he'd go as far away as Yangon? He never leaves his monastery. He never accepts invitations."

"My dear fellow," U Boon Shein said, "I don't know anything about all that. It doesn't concern me. My duty is to simply go to the Sayadaw and convey the message my teacher gave me. The Sayadaw can tell me himself whether he will accept the invitation to come to Yangon or not. Please just arrange for me to have a car to go to Kyauksai as quickly as possible!"

The car was arranged and U Boon Shein approached Ven. Webu Sayadaw around lunch time. In those days, the Sayadaw was not surrounded by crowds of people making offerings when he had his meals—there were only two lay nuns, three or four lay women, and two attendants present. The lay disciples and the attendants, named U Kyaung and Bo Tun, served the Sayadaw every day.

"I have come with a message from Sayagyi U Ba Khin, venerable sir," U Boon Shein told Ven. Webu Sayadaw. The Sayadaw looked up from his bowl, glanced at U Boon Shein, and said, "Yes, yes," then continued his meal. When U Boon Shein looked at the Sayadaw's face, he had the impression the Sayadaw was saying, "Yes, I knew you were coming. Wait for a moment." U Boon Shein waited humbly.

After finishing his meal, Ven. Webu Sayadaw glanced at U Boon Shein. "Have you come all the way from Yangon, lay disciple?" he asked.

"That is correct, sir. I was sent by the great lay disciple U Ba Khin."

"The great lay disciple U Ba Khin?"

"Yes, sir. He is the great disciple who came to Webu to pay respects to you before the war. That was in the month of Wagaung in 1302 (1941). Because of your instructions to him, he has been teaching meditation and spreading the Dhamma ever since. After the war, U Ba Khin became Accountant General of Burma and has settled down in Yangon. He teaches meditation to his subordinates in a meditation room in his office. There are also some foreigners who practice meditation under his guidance and who have become Buddhists."

"It is delightful to hear that he is sharing the Dhamma he obtained through his unwavering effort in the practice," Ven. Webu Sayadaw said.

"Yes, sir. Accountant General U Ba Khin founded the Vipassanā Research Association in 1951 together with some of his office workers. He has been studying their meditation experiences in a scientific manner. He has compiled a small booklet of his findings entitled The Basic Study of the Buddha's Teachings and Their Correct Application, and he wishes to submit it to you for your approval. Thanks to your loving kindness and encouragement, he was able to found the Vipassanā Association on the new-moon day of Kason in 1951, and all the employees of the Accountant General's Office were given permission to join. These office workers' families also wanted to join, so the space in the shrine room at the office was too small. As a result, we bought a plot of land on Inya Myaing Road. A meditation centre was opened there on the new-moon day of Kason in 1952, and Sayagyi is teaching at the new centre. He has built a Dhamma Yaung Chi Ceti on a small hill at the centre, and his main concern now is teaching the Dhamma to foreigners."

Ven. Webu Sayadaw looked at U Boon Shein with loving kindness as he gave this explanation without asking any questions. Then U Boon Shein conveyed Sayagyi U Ba Khin's message. "There is a pagoda at the centre now," he said, "with eight meditation cells. We have also built living quarters for you to live in and a Dhamma Hall. Sayagyi has sent me to you to humbly request that out of compassion for us you travel to Yangon to bless the Dhamma Yaung Chi Ceti, which was built about a year ago."

The two attendants and the ladies looked at U Boon Shein and the Sayadaw doubtfully when he said this, but U Boon Shein continued, "I have a special message from Sayagyi U Ba Khin to convey to you, sir: The people of Kyauksai, Shwebo, and Khin U are able to pay respects to the qualities of *sīla*, *samādhi*, and *paññā* as embodied by the Venerable Sayadaw, but there are many people in other parts of Burma who cannot easily obtain an opportunity to pay respects to the Sayadaw. Your *pāramīs* are very powerful and your ability to teach is very great. The places where people have received this Teaching from you are very few. Venerable sir, the great disciple U Ba Khin requests that you leave your monasteries and that, with your great loving kindness (*mettā*) and compassion (*karuṇā*), you tour the country in order to dispense the cooling Dhamma to all the people of Burma. He says that now is a good time for the Sayadaw to do so."

U Boon Shein had finished his short speech. He wiped the sweat from his brow with his handkerchief and waited for the Sayadaw's reply. Everyone in the little bamboo hut was silent.

"When do you want us to come to Yangon?" the Sayadaw's voice broke the silence.

"Whenever you wish, sir," U Boon Shein answered with a trembling voice.

"Well, I don't think we can leave tomorrow," Ven. Webu Sayadaw said, "so it will have to be the day after tomorrow. Does it suit you if we come the day after tomorrow?"

U Boon Shein was so happy he could hardly speak. "It … it is suitable, sir," he said. "I'll inform Yangon immediately so that everything can be made ready."

The Sayadaw sent Bo Tun to fetch two monks, U Ñāṇa and U Sumana. When they arrived, he said, "We are going to Yangon to instruct the disciples there. Arrange everything for the journey with his lay disciple. We will go with six monks and two attendants."

The two monks were so surprised they could scarcely believe their ears. They went outside and asked U Boon Shein to explain. Then they conferred on the arrangements for the trip to Yangon. The date was Friday, July 3, 1953. They agreed that the trip would be made by plane on Sunday, July 5th. U Boon Shein went back into the Sayadaw's hut to pay respects and to inform him of the arrangements.

"The Sayadaw and his disciples will travel by plane to Yangon on Sunday," he said. "Please inform your disciple of any special requirements for your stay in Yangon."

"Just ask the great disciple in Yangon to provide toilet facilities in accordance with the Vinaya rules for the monks," Ven. Webu Sayadaw said. "There's nothing else we need."

U Boon Shein went back to Mandalay and headed straight for the telephone exchange in order to call Yangon. As the Accountant General's Office was one of the most important government departments, U Boon Shein was able to speak to Sayagyi and convey the good news to him in no time. He then went to his friend's office to tell him what had happened. His friend was very surprised. U Boon Shein waited in his friend's office to hear from Sayagyi. Within an hour, he was told that everything had been arranged. Tickets had been bought and places booked on the plane for the monks, the lay disciples, and U Boon Shein. They would be leaving Mandalay on Sunday at noon, arriving in Yangon at 2:30 P.M. They would be met at the airport.

At the International Meditation Centre in Yangon, preparations for the Sayadaw and his followers were quickly made: their living quarters, robes, the toilet facilities, etc.

Ven. Webu Sayadaw was brought to the Centre from the airport in a large car. The people who were there to welcome him took their places on either side of the flight of steps leading to the pagoda and on the pagoda platform. When the car stopped at the bottom of the steps, Sayagyi opened the door himself. After he got out of the car, Ven. Webu Sayadaw looked up at the pagoda, which had recently been gilded and crowned with its *hri* (parasol). It was shining and sparkling in the sunlight. The Sayadaw stopped at the foot of the steps and raised his hands towards the pagoda in veneration. Only after doing this did he slowly proceed up the steps towards the pagoda platform.

When they arrived at the pagoda platform, Sayagyi raised his joined hands in reverence and indicated the way. They circumambulated the pagoda three times, keeping it to their right, then Sayagyi invited the Sayadaw to enter the pagoda through the north cell. The Sayadaw entered the central room.[9] Sayagyi U Ba Khin's disciples were seated in the cells around the central room and all around the pagoda outside, and they raised their joined hands in respect to the Sayadaw. They paid their respects, fixing their minds on the Dhamma.

Sayagyi then said, "This Dhamma Yaung Chi Ceti is a place where the three Noble Gems of the Buddha, the Dhamma, and the Saṅgha can be worshipped and our debt of gratitude to them can be repaid. It is a place that we have established in order that it can be the centre of our teaching of the paths and the fruits to the world, making the qualities of *sīla*, *samādhi*, and *paññā* the basis of our teaching. Venerable Webu Sayadaw has made the journey here to give us the necessary strength and protection and to instruct us. After we take the precepts (*sīla*) from him, we will fix our minds on the aspects of the Dhamma we have realized, we will pay respects to the Buddha, to Venerable Webu Sayadaw, and to the monks accompanying him. May Sakka, the king of the *devas*, the Four Guardians of the World, and all the great *deva* princes descend on this place! May they join us in the highest meritorious deed of paying respects to the Buddha, the Dhamma, and the Saṅgha, and may they protect us!"

Everyone then took the Triple Refuge and the moral precepts from Ven. Webu Sayadaw, and this was followed by everyone paying their respects by meditating for five minutes.

Sayagyi gave a talk, relating how he had first met and paid respects to Ven. Webu Sayadaw in 1941. He said he had started to teach after Webu Sayadaw urged him to do so. Sayagyi spoke of how he had founded the Accountant General's Vipassanā Research Association and of how he taught meditation to the office staff and to foreigners, who had become Buddhists through this. The site on Inya Myaing Road had been acquired after the Association was well established and the Dhamma Yaung Chi Ceti was built there. The International Meditation Centre was founded at this location in order to spread the Buddha-Dhamma throughout the world.

As Sayagyi spoke, Ven. Webu Sayadaw's face was lit by a smile. It was obvious from his expression that he was happy with what he heard.

Sayagyi continued, repeating the message he had given to U Boon Shein to take to the Sayadaw in Kyauksai. He explained to Webu Sayadaw that lay people were giving their support to the study of the Buddha's Teachings (*pariyatti-sāsana*) by providing the four requisites for the monks, who preserve the texts, and by arranging exams on the Pāḷi texts. He spoke of the strenuous efforts being made to establish *vipassanā* meditation centres so that the study of the Buddha's Teachings and the practice of the Buddha's Teachings (*pariyatti-sāsana*) could grow. The government wanted to support the Sāsana by convening the Sixth Buddhist Council.

Sayagyi then said that the power of Ven. Webu Sayadaw's *sīla*, *samādhi*, and *paññā* was very great and that the Sayadaw would be of great importance in strengthening the Sāsana. Up until then, however, only the people in Kyauksai, Shwebo, and Khin U had been able to benefit from the Sayadaw's uplifting loving kindness (*mettā*). Throughout Myanmar, Sayagyi said, there were many beings who possessed the perfections (*pāramī*) and the Sayadaw should look on them with his great compassion, for the time had come for those who were practicing the Buddha's Teachings to become well established in them. He requested the Sayadaw to teach the Dhamma and to spread the Dhamma from the Dhamma Yaung Chi Ceti during this auspicious period.

After Sayagyi finished, Ven. Webu Sayadaw said, "The practice of the Great Teacher's Teachings leads to the appeasing of suffering. You all know this for yourselves. It is very noble to pass one's own Dhamma on to others. This is the noblest gift of all. You know the gratitude you owe to the Buddha. You practice the Dhamma. This practice is the highest practice. You are all doing noble work in an auspicious place. As a result, you will obtain great benefits. The results of your efforts will be in accordance with the strength of your *pāramī*. Establish yourselves through the power of effort and continue to practice according to the Buddha's instructions. In this way you will attain everything that should be attained. We came here in answer to your invitation so that we would not be lacking in repaying our debt to the Buddha, so that we could pay back the debt of gratitude we have to the Buddha. In olden days, those who were wise also worked in this way, being constantly mindful, and they attained their goal. In the same way, Noble Ones today succeed through establishing effort and working hard."

All those present were delighted and said, "*Sādhu*, *sādhu*, *sādhu*," with great devotion and joyful voices.

Afterwards, Webu Sayadaw was taken to his quarters in a building that had been set up as a temporary monastery, and all the monks with him were given their own accommodation. At six o'clock in the evening, cold drinks were offered to the Sayadaw and the monks, and after that, the Sayadaw gave a talk to the people who had come from Yangon to pay respects. It was only the following day that a multitude of visitors from all over the city came to the centre. The visitors included former President Saw Shwe Thaik, judges, and government ministers. They all brought offerings of food, robes, and other requisites. Ven. Webu Sayadaw gave three discourses each day to the people who came to pay respects.

At that time, there were also meditation students at the centre. Sayagyi looked after them and made sure that they received the Teachings. Ven. Webu Sayadaw had his monks meditate in the cells in the pagoda, and he himself meditated in the central room every morning and evening, filling the pagoda with Bodhi-*dhātu*, Dhamma-*dhātu*, and Nibbāna-*dhātu*.

In this way, the people of Yangon were able to pay respects to Webu Sayadaw and receive the Teachings from him for seven days. They had this opportunity thanks to Sayagyi's concern, loving kindness, and foresight, and thanks to the efforts of the members of the Vipassanā Association. So the people of Yangon are greatly indebted to them for this.

After the seven days were over, Ven. Webu Sayadaw and the monks accompanying him returned to Kyauksai by train, taking with them the many gifts offered in Yangon.

When people heard that Ven. Webu Sayadaw had visited the International Meditation Centre, they wanted to have him come to their own villages, towns, and regions. In Yangon, former President Saw Shwe Thaik formed an association that was to organize the Sayadaw's visits to the capital. They invited him to come in May 1954. While staying at the association's temporary monastery, Ven. Webu Sayadaw went to I.M.C. on May 1st and meditated with Sayagyi and his disciples in the Dhamma Yaung Chi Ceti. That afternoon, he gave them a talk in the centre's Dhamma Hall at five o'clock, and they made suitable offerings to him at that time.

After that, Ven. Webu Sayadaw came to Yangon each year at the association's invitation. He visited I.M.C. again on May 10, 1955; Feb. 21, 1957; and April 5, 1958. On each of these visits he meditated with Sayagyi and his disciples in the Dhamma Yaung Chi Ceti and then gave a talk in the Dhamma Hall. The members of the Vipassanā Association always made an offering of robes and the other requisites for monks.

In 1960, seven years after the Sayadaw's first visit to I.M.C., Sayagyi sent him the following letter:

The Vipassanā Association
Office of the Accountant General
Yangon, Myanmar
(The 15th day of the new moon
of Natdaw, 1321/Dec. 14, 1959)

Maung Ba Khin respectfully addresses Venerable Webu Sayadaw!

Since the month of Wagaung 1302 [August 1940], when your disciple first met the Venerable Sayadaw while on a tour in the service of the Railways Accounts Department, your disciple has undertaken many tasks and duties in the service of the Sāsana, following the Venerable Sayadaw's admonition. The Venerable Sayadaw has seen for himself the Dhamma Yaung Chi Ceti and the success of our work at our meditation centre. He has seen the many foreigners from all over the world who have been given the Dhamma by his disciple.

In 1315 (June 1953), the Venerable Sayadaw came to the meditation centre in Inya Myaing Road and resided there for exactly seven days. During that time, the Sayadaw gave the cooling medicine of the Deathless. The Sayadaw will also remember that, having sown very special seeds for the Sāsana, he began to actively spread the Teachings.

Since that time, over six years ago, the Venerable Sayadaw has travelled to many places all over Myanmar and has benefited beings beyond measure. Your disciples can also say that their work has progressed satisfactorily.

As we are entering the seventh year since the Venerable Sayadaw first visited us, your disciple requests that you honour the International Meditation Centre with your presence together with your Saṅgha for a period of ten days for the benefit and development of the Sāsana, for the benefit and development of beings, and in order to bring inspiration. If the Sayadaw wishes to come, everything will be according to the Sayadaw's wishes.

The Sayadaw's disciples, who are full of hope, respectfully request the Sayadaw to come to I.M.C. for ten days, for this meditation centre is very dear to the Sayadaw, who, out of great compassion and great loving kindness, strives to make the Sāsana continue to grow. If he should come, the disciples under his protection and guidance, both monks and lay people, will have an opportunity to savour the extraordinary taste of the Dhamma (*dhamma-rasa*). Therefore, your disciples earnestly and humbly request the Sayadaw to favour us with his visit.

Maung Ba Khin
The International Meditation Centre
Inya Myaing Road, Yangon

Ven. Webu Sayadaw was not able to reside at the centre for ten days, however, as he had accepted other invitations. But he did come for five days (May 13–18, 1960). Once again, those at the centre were able to pay respects to the Sayadaw as they had done before. There was also an American, Dr. Hislop, at the centre at that time. He had been meditating there for nearly a month and was able to continue while Ven. Webu Sayadaw was there. Dr. Hislop took the Triple Refuge from the Sayadaw. Ven. Webu Sayadaw was very happy about this and urged Sayagyi to teach more foreigners. On the last day of his visit, he made this the main topic of his talk. "I also started teaching at this place," he said over and over again.

U Ko Lay's Account of Sayagyi's Ordination

At about half past four, we arrived at Webu Sayadaw's monastery, the Ingyinbin forest retreat, in Khin U township. The sky had been overcast during the entire trip, so we were spared the oppressive heat and arrived at the monastery feeling fresh.

We immediately informed U Sumana (the Sayadaw's nephew, the monk in charge of the refectory) of our arrival and the reason for our visit. He went to report to Webu Sayadaw. Sayagyi and I were lodged in a new building donated by the rice mill owners U Ba Tu and Daw Hymin.[10] That evening at about seven o'clock, the Pauk Taw Sayadaw U Sāsana ordained Sayagyi and me as *sāmaṇeras* (novices), and at about eight o'clock, we went to pay respects to Webu Sayadaw. We requested the Sayadaw to be our preceptor and accept us as his disciples. The Sayadaw asked Sayagyi the day of the week he was born[1] and whether he remembered the name he had been given at his ordination as a *sāmaṇera* when he was a boy. Sayagyi replied that he was born on a Monday and that the Shway-gon-taing Sayadaw had given him the name U Kusala when he ordained as a novice.

"This is a name well suited to you, great lay disciple," the Sayadaw said. "You will take this name as a monk, also."

As I could not remember my monk's name from my former ordination, the Sayadaw pondered for a while and then said, "As you were born on Saturday, I'll give you the name Ashin Tejinda."

On Friday, June 18, 1965, a group of lay disciples assembled in the Dhamma Hall after nine o'clock to pay respects to the Sayadaw. After giving a discourse, Webu Sayadaw had the ordination ceremony prepared. As on the last occasion when I had ordained, the men from the village that offered alms to the monastery put the future monks under a palanquin and carried them on their shoulders around the boundaries of the monastery. In the procession behind the men came the women, carrying palm leaves and flowers. Drums and other musical instruments were played. After this, Sayagyi had alms food offered to over fifty monks and novices.

At about one o'clock, Sayagyi and I (both still *sāmaṇeras*) had to go to the Sīmā (ordination hall) that was in front of the Tiloka Sabbaññu Ceti to take part in the ordination ceremony with the local Saṅgha. When Webu Sayadaw came, we became *dullabha* bhikkhus[12] under him and entered the folds of the Sāsana. The reciters of the *kammavācā* (a formal proceeding; in this case, the ordination) were Sayadaw U Sāsana from Pauktaw Monastery, U Āsara from Sawgyi Monastery, Sayadaw U Ñāṇa from the Webu Meditation Monastery, U Sumana from Ingyinbin Monastery, and many others. We became monks at 2:06 P.M. Because the sky had been overcast since that morning, it was not possible to measure a man's shadow to determine the time of day.[13]

Thanks to the Buddha, the Knower of the Three Worlds, the Omniscient One, in the year 2509 of the Buddhist religion, the year 1327 by the Burmese calendar, on the fourth day of the waning moon in the month of Nayon, a Thursday, at two hours and six minutes after noon, we were ordained under the Sayadaw of Ingyinbin Monastery before the *kammavācā* experts and qualified Saṅghas (monks) who were eighteen in all. Ashin Kusala and Ashin Tejinda were lifted from the lowly state of novices to the lofty state of monkhood.

At four o'clock, having become monks, we moved from our house in the section of the monastery reserved for lay people, to a building in the part reserved for monks. The building was called Yan-aung-mingalar-kyaung ("the auspicious monastery for the overcoming of danger"). It had been donated by U Aung, Daw Yin, and their family, who were from Market Street in the Shantaw quarter in Monywa. The building was a new, single storey structure, and U Kusala and U Tejinda were the first monks to occupy it.[14] As there was running water, we had a flush toilet and a bathroom. We also had electricity. Sayagyi (U Kusala) lived in the front room near the entrance and I was in the back near the bathroom. U Hla Tun stayed in a small meditation hut at the back of our building. He prepared our early morning meal there.

At 5:00 P.M., we went to the Tipiṭaka Library to pay respects to the Sayadaw with all the other monks. Then at 6:00 P.M., we went to see the Sayadaw in his residence and Sayagyi made an offering of the following items: one set of the Piṭaka texts, five sets of robes, five umbrellas, five pairs of slippers, and five blankets.

Saturday, June 19, 1965, was our first day as monks. We followed the same timetable that is used during meditation courses at the International Meditation Centre in Inya Myaing Road, Yangon. I got up just before four o'clock in the morning. I do not know how long Sayagyi had already been up by then. I found him sitting cross-legged on his bed, meditating.

After eating our dawn meal, which consisted of rice mixed with sundry ingredients, we continued to meditate in our monastery. Then Sayagyi went to water a young Bodhi tree, and he recited the Udāna and Paṭṭhāna.[15] He awakened the Bodhi-*dhātu* (the element of Awakening). After our midday meal at eleven o'clock, we continued to meditate, following the same schedule used at IMC-Yangon. From five to nine in the evening we took exercise, walking up and down, and then went to see the Sayadaw. We paid respects to him and performed our duties towards him. From nine to eleven, we meditated and then went to bed. We observed this schedule every day and I believe that in this way my observance of the monks' rules was more perfect than the first time I was there.

Sayagyi spent a great deal of time reciting verses of the Udāna, the Uddesa and Niddesa of the Paṭṭhāna, the Paṭṭhānapaññāvāra, and the Mahāsamaya-sutta, either in the shade of the Bodhi tree or in our monastery.

One Sunday, June 20, 1965, we went for a walk around the monastery boundary after our meal at dawn. We found Ven. Webu Sayadaw walking up and down. He was holding a broom in his hand, and whenever he saw some rubbish, he swept it up. He especially swept under some flowering trees where the ground was covered with withered blossoms.

At about twenty past seven, the Sayadaw came to our building. There were lay people sweeping all around the monastery. The Sayadaw came into our monastery and stood there as we paid respects to him. He did not speak at first. His eyes looked around the room. Then he looked at us.

"Is everything well with you?" he asked. "Are you developing understanding?"

Sayagyi told him that he wished to donate three hundred kyats towards a pagoda to be built at Webu Sayadaw's birthplace, and two hundred kyats for repairs to the Buddha seats under the Bodhi trees. Sayagyi also said he would send flowering trees for the monastery. Webu Sayadaw accepted these offerings and left us again.

Our time of arrival coincided exactly with the beginning of preparations to build a pagoda at the spot where Webu Sayadaw was born.[16] This was in the village of Ingyinbin. If one follows the road in front of the monastery gate, one arrives after a short while in Ingyinbin. The former site of the house of the Sayadaw's family is to the north of the village, against the boundary fence. This is where the Shwe-chet-tho Ceti[17] was built for the Sayadaw.

The Sayadaw had three Bodhi trees planted in the compound of the meditation centre. The one in the north-west corner was already quite big. The other two were planted later. Sayagyi gave *dāna* so that the surrounding walls and the Buddha seats under these two trees could be repaired.

On Monday, June 22, 1965, Sayagyi went to pay respects to the monks who accompanied Webu Sayadaw whenever he came to IMC-Yangon. At 3.00 A.M. that morning, the Sayadaw, accompanied by a few monks, went to the place where the new pagoda was to be built. He recited the Parittas and marked the site with a post. In the afternoon, the villagers cleared the ground for the foundations of the pagoda under the guidance of U Sumana (the monk who was Webu Sayadaw's nephew).

From a quarter past eight until after nine o'clock on June 24, we had the opportunity to spend some time alone with the Sayadaw. Sayagyi told Webu Sayadaw that we would disrobe and go back to Yangon the next day because he had to fulfil his responsibilities towards his disciples, especially the foreign disciples. If the opportunity arose, Sayagyi continued, he planned to go abroad to teach meditation. He requested the Sayadaw to give him advice concerning the spreading of the Teachings in foreign countries. The Sayadaw complied with this request and explained the aspects that required special attention.

Then I told the Sayadaw how I started practicing Ānāpāna when I first ordained, and how I had continued to meditate, first under Shwe-zedi Sayadaw, then under Sayagyi U Ba Khin. "But venerable sir," I continued, "there is one thing that is not clear to me. I have been working hard in this field of meditation for many years now, but if I compare my mind with other people's minds, I have not developed greatly. I wonder if I have any *pāramīs*?"

The Sayadaw listened attentively to what I had to say and then replied, "You have *pāramīs*, and they are not few. You have a great many *pāramīs*. Look at these other people," he said, pointing to three or four people from the village who were sweeping outside. "Their *pāramīs* are only a few, but yours are many. You live now in a big brick building with a nice garden around it. I don't mean the house you were living in before. That didn't belong to you. I mean the house and garden in which you are living now. You have flowers and trees. You own many things. These people don't have all that. If you listen to the Lord Buddha's Teachings and practice them, then you will attain anything you aspire to."

I did not have much time to think about his words as we had to make arrangements for the offering Sayagyi was going to present to all the monks,

Webu Sayadaw followed by U Kusala (Sayagyi U Ba Khin) and U Tejinda (U Ko Lay), Ingyinbin Monastry

novices, and *sīla-shins*[18] at the monastery. We first took food to Webu Sayadaw and offered it to him. After that, food was offered to the other residents of the monastery.

It was only when I lay down after the midday meal that I started to wonder how the Sayadaw could possibly have known that I now owned my own house and garden. He had been to my house in the compound of Mandalay University. I had told him about moving to Maymyo, but nothing else. What did the Sayadaw want to tell me by comparing my situation with that of the people from the village, saying I had good *pāramīs*?

After taking rest, I sat on my bed meditating. After a while I opened my eyes. I looked through to the other room where Sayagyi was sitting cross-legged reciting the Paṭṭhāna. Behind his head I could see Webu Sayadaw's dwelling. I understood then that the Sayadaw had wanted to tell me not to look only at people of eminent *pāramīs* such as himself and Sayagyi, but also to compare myself with people of few *pāramīs* in order to see how far I had already come. That was why he had pointed out the village men who were sweeping the compound.

In the evening, we went back for the last time with the other monks to pay respects to Webu Sayadaw. Sayagyi then went to water the Bodhi tree. Afterwards, he recited the Udāna until nine o'clock.

After having our meal at dawn on June 28th, we reverted to the lower state of laymen in the presence of the Sayadaw. We tidied up our things and cleaned our living quarters with the help of U Hla Tun. Then we greeted U Sumana and the other monks who were there and left the Ingyinbin forest retreat.

We stopped in Khin U to collect our pictures, which had been taken by a photographer from a studio there a few days before. From there, we continued to Shwebo where we stopped at U Hpe Tin's house for coffee and a snack. Then we went to Webu Sayadaw's monastery outside Shwebo to pay respects and look around. We continued our journey and arrived at eleven o'clock at the Kaung-hmudaw Pagoda. We circumambulated the pagoda twice and made offerings of flowers, oil lamps, and incense. Back in Sagaing, we rested and had lunch at my wife's sisters' house.

We did not continue straight to Maymyo, but went to Kyauksai. We went to the Webu Monastery outside the town. When Sayagyi paid respects at the residence of Webu Sayadaw at the top of a hill it started to rain gently. In this light drizzle, we descended back into the valley and went to the place where Sayagyi had first paid respects to the Sayadaw twenty-four years before. Then, as Sayagyi paid respects at the pagoda, the Bodhi tree, and the residence, it began to rain more heavily.

After this we went to pay respects to a monk named Shin Saw Lu. Every time I went to the Kyauksai Monastery, I went to see Venerable Shin Saw

Lu. He is a monk of exceptional composure and is steadfast in the practice of meditation. He is the only monk who stayed at the Sīmā after listening to the Sayadaw's admonitions and quietly meditating for the whole night. When Ven. Webu Sayadaw came to the Dhamma Yaung Chi Ceti at IMC-Yangon, Sayagyi paid special attention to Ven. Shin Saw Lu and respected him for his efforts. When we came out after having paid respects to Shin Saw Lu Sayadaw, it had stopped raining and the sun was coming out again. The clouds dispersed and the weather became pleasant and fine. When we reached Mandalay, the sun was shining brilliantly.

The sky had been overcast from nine o'clock in the morning on June 17th (when we left Maymyo to go to Ingyinbin) until the end of our ten days as monks (when we left Kyauksai). The sun had shone for only a few short moments during that time. I remember clearly how the sun came through after a heavy downpour at the end of our journey in Kyauksai.

We left Mandalay at 5:30 in the afternoon and arrived in Maymyo at 7:46 P.M. Sayagyi agreed to rest at my house for a day in order to give inspiration to my family. During this day, Sayagyi spent most of the time in our Buddha shrine, meditating and reciting the Paṭṭhāna.

On June 30th, after lunch, I took Sayagyi to Mandalay and we arrived at the train station before two o'clock. With the help of Ko Ohn, an accountant who knew Sayagyi well, we bought a seat reservation and a ticket at the station. Though Sayagyi's train left on time, he arrived an hour late in Yangon the next morning as the train had to stop in Pyinmana for an hour due to some technical problem.

Sayagyi was in the habit of keeping a diary. In it, he gives a detailed account of this period when, for the only time in his life, he was able to become a *dullabha* bhikkhu. I am able to give so many details about this time in Ingyinbin only because I had access to Sayagyi's notes.

There is an entry in the diary under July 6th that is entitled: "The journey to the Ingyinbin forest monastery in Khin U township in Shwebo District to pay respects and to venerate Webu Sayadaw." He gave the text of this entry to his disciples:

When I arrived in the presence of the Sayadaw, I venerated him, not only with material gifts, but I also venerated him by entering the folds of the Saṅgha, by observing the exalted Vinaya rules of the monks, and by practicing meditation in this lofty Dhamma. The giving of *dāna* I practiced was also a perfection of *dāna* I had not practiced before in this life.[19] As the Association and all the disciples take part in this giving of *dāna* as well, I went in front of the Sayadaw after I had reverted to lay life and shared the merits in his presence and with his *mettā* blessings.

The Kusala Actions[20]

Dāna-kusala [Merit through generosity]

for Ingyinbin Pagoda	K	300.—
for Bodhi tree walls	K	200.—
for Kaung-hmudaw Pagoda	K	20.—
3 sets of the Tipi(t)aka in Burmese	K	684.—
2 sets of three robes	K	190.—
3 sets of two robes	K	240.—
5 umbrellas	K	40.—
6 pairs of sandals	K	96.—
2 leather seats	K	10.—
2 bowls and strainers, etc.	K	37.—
1 razor	K	13.—
candles and incense sticks	K	20.—
1 big box of cakes	K	32.—
Two days of food offerings		
(1) June 18, 1965 K		300.—
(2) June 27, 1965 K		500.—
Total	K	2442.—

Note: In the food cost are included K 220 from the Vipassanā Association. Apart from the above items, mangoes, mangosteen, and savoury snacks were offered by my Indian disciples.

Sīla-kusala [Merit through morality]

Having entered the sublime state of being a bhikkhu, I observed the 227 rules of conduct with respect and diligence. I made a special effort not to infringe even the minor rules of conduct. In this lifetime, I had the opportunity to practice this high type of *Sīla* only during these ten days of monkhood.

Bhāvanā-kusala [Merit through developing the mind]

Whenever I was free from my duties towards the Buddha, the Dhamma, and the Saṅgha, I directed my mind towards the Dhamma, and in this way, showed my respect by meditating, by practicing *paṭipatti* [putting the Teachings into practice].

Daily schedule

After eating the dawn meal, I offered water to the Bodhi tree and then recited the Udāna [the Awakening of the Buddha in three stages][21] in its shade.Back at my lodgings, I recited the Uddesa and Niddesa of the Paṭṭhāna.[22] At midday, I paid homage by reciting the Paṭṭhāna Pañhāvāra.[23] At four o'clock in the afternoon, I showed reverence by reciting the Mahāsamaya-*sutta* along with the other six *suttas* that were taught on the Great Occasion.[24] Before nine in the evening, I recited the Udāna Gāthās, the Anekajāti saísāraí,[25] and other Gāthās under the Bodhi tree and then remained there meditating until exactly nine o'clock.

The *dāna-kusala*, *sīla-kusala*, *bhāvanā-kusala* that I performed, together with the merit I gained by revering the Buddha, the Dhamma, and the Saṅgha, I share with all the *Brahmās*, *devas*, and humans who help me in the perfection of my *pāramīs*, and especially with those of the Vipassanā Association who take responsibility in helping in the spreading of the *paṭipatti-sāsana*.

May all be happy in mind and body. May they be filled with the wisdom pertaining to the paths (*magga*) and fruition states (*phala*). May they attain to the Awakening (*bodhi*) to which they aspire.

Sayagyi U Ba Khin, President
Vipassanā Association
31A Inya Myaing Road
July 6, 1965

Comments

BY SAYAGYI U CHIT TIN

A. At that time, Sayagyi was the Chairman of the Sub-committee for Paṭipatti at the Buddha Sāsana Council, Yangon, Myanmar. He was assigned the task of settling the issues concerning the meditation centres in the country. The reports received at the Council from these centres said that there were a large number of path and fruition state winners ranging from teenage girls to elderly people. The Executive Committee was comprised of twenty-seven members who were well-known religious people from all over the country. Most of them were learned or popular Pāḷi scholars. They were all concerned that there might be something wrong at the centres, but they did not dare criticize them since it would be very harmful to say anything against the Dhamma.

In order to resolve the issue, the Executive Committee had the papers transferred to the Sub-committee for Paṭipatti Affairs chaired by Sayagyi. All this occurred in 1953. Sayagyi had to look for a solution that would not disappoint anyone. He wrote The Basic Study of the Buddha's Teachings and their Correct Application in Burmese and submitted it to his Sub-committee and later to the Executive Committee. A resolution was passed to distribute it to all the meditation centres in the country for their response. No replies came from any of the centres, not even those that had sent in lists of path and fruition state winners. After that, no more of these lists were sent. Sayagyi sent his printed pamphlet to Webu Sayadaw separately, through the Deputy Comptroller of Accounts for Burma Railways, U Bo Lay, whose mother was one of the Sayadaw's lay supporters. U Maung Maung (an ex-colonel) who meditated with Sayamagyi in 1984 and who now stays at IMC-Yangon most of the time, is U Bo Lay's younger brother.

B. It was not surprising to Sayagyi and his immediate disciples that the Sayadaw should accept Sayagyi's invitation. One night, after the day's work of teaching and group sittings were over, Sayagyi was inspired by an idea. So he told Sayamagyi and Sayagyi U Chit Tin to enter the pagoda cells. Sayagyi instructed Sayamagyi to prepare herself and then he mentally invited the Sayadaw.

Sayagyi and Sayamagyi came out of the Pagoda and Sayagyi instructed U Boon Shein, the treasurer of the centre's Vipassanā Association, to fly to Mandalay the next day. From there he was to proceed by car to Kyauksai Webu Chaung to give Webu Sayadaw a formal invitation. This incident was remembered by many of Sayagyi's disciples, including Sao Shwe Thaik, who had been the first president of Myanmar. Sao Shwe Thaik was asked later on to chair the Yangon Committee that invited Webu Sayadaw to Lower

Myanmar for annual visits, starting the next year. He told how he asked the Sayadaw when he had a chance to talk with him privately, "Can someone mentally invite another person?" Sao Shwe Thaik had heard that Sayagyi had mentally invited the Sayadaw and that the Sayadaw had given his consent; then U Boon Shein had been sent to make a formal invitation. "Lay disciple," Webu Sayadaw replied immediately, "if the purity is there, it can happen at a certain stage."

After Ven. Webu Sayadaw came to the Centre, Sayagyi invited Sao Shwe Thaik to come and pay respects to the Sayadaw. Sao Shwe Thaik came at about seven o'clock on his way to a dinner party. He asked the Sayadaw if he and Sayagyi taught the same thing. He also asked if he should meditate under Sayagyi, and the Sayadaw told him he should. Sao Shwe Thaik immediately requested Sayagyi to teach him, so they both took leave of the Sayadaw and went into the pagoda. Sayagyi assigned Sao Shwe Thaik the south cell, the one in which the Buddha statue was installed about a year later. Then Sayagyi taught him Ānāpāna meditation. Sao Shwe Thaik had said that he only had one hour before the dinner party, but he remained seated for two hours. Sayagyi opened the door between the cell and the central shrine room after the two hours and Sao Shwe Thaik opened his eyes. He was surprised that he had sat for such a long time. Now he was late for his dinner party, but he was so impressed by the meditation, he said, "Never mind, I won't go now." After this, the south cell was given to elderly men.

C. As usual, Sayagyi recounted his experiences when he returned to IMC-Yangon. Sayamagyi may have been there, but no one else was present when he told Sayagyi U Chit Tin of an extraordinary incident at Webu Sayadaw's monastery. In the late afternoon on June 17, 1965, the day of their arrival, while U Hla Tun was shaving Sayagyi's head, the Sayadaw suddenly arrived, squatted in front of Sayagyi, and started picking up the hair that had been shaved off his head. He collected some and went away. Sayagyi was amazed at this, and he told U Hla Tun to save some of the hair in an empty plastic medicine bottle that Sayagyi took back to Yangon with him. He always kept this bottle behind the Buddha statue in the IMC Pagoda. When Sayamagyi and Sayagyi U Chit Tin came out of Myanmar, they brought half of the hair with them so that the hair could be honoured and revered. The hair is now enshrined in the Dhamma Yaung Chi Cetis that have been built all around the world for the benefit of many.

D. As the building had just been completed, the building compound needed to be cleaned and the footpath to the main entrance laid out. Even though it was late in the evening, Ven. Webu Sayadaw assembled some lay disciples to help clear the grounds and make this footpath. The main entrance of the house was in the middle of the compound and the footpath led directly to Ven. Webu Sayadaw's monastery. The path is called the Min-lan-ma or "The King's Highway."

U Hla Tun was there helping the men working on the main path, but he thought the side footpaths that had been used by the workers and tradesmen during the construction of the building would serve for one night. Sayagyi overheard him thinking out loud and decided to admonish him with a few questions.

"How would the *brahmās* and *devas* approach the monastery?" he asked. "Would they come by the side paths or by the King's Highway?"

"They will come by the King's Highway, reverend sir," U Hla Htun replied.

"Yes," Sayagyi said. "Just as a king would take the Min-lan-ma, so too should the bhikkhus and *sāmaṅeras*. What has to be done should be done immediately. There is no time to waste. It should be done properly, working cooperatively and in harmony with your co-workers."[26]

E. Sayagyi collected a selection of texts from the Tipiṭaka (Pāḷi Canon) and had them published in a booklet on the Buddha's Day (the full-moon day of the month of Kason), 1313 Burmese Era (May 20, 1951). The texts were: Udāna, Paṭicca-samuppāda, Uddesa, Niddesa, Aṭṭhajaya-maṅgalā-gāthā (Dhammapada, vv. 153–54, "The verses celebrating the eightfold victory"). This booklet was printed as Dhamma-dāna. The Buddha-Sāsana Akyosaung Athin of the Accountant General's Office distributed it free of charge. According to Ven. Ledi Sayadaw, these texts, if learnt by heart and recited daily throughout one's life, make the body resemble a Dhamma-ceti, and men and *devas* will gain merit by worshipping and revering the reciter of the verses. Sayagyi solemnly declared that by reciting these verses with a faithful heart and a concentrated mind, visualizing the Buddha attaining Buddhahood, it is possible to awaken the Bodhi-dhātu. A note reproducing Ledi Sayadaw's words was added in the booklet after the Udāna Niddesa.

F. After becoming a monk on Friday, June 18, 1965, Sayagyi realized that the Sayadaw desired to build a pagoda at his birthplace, nearly one kilometre north of the meditation centre. That same night, Sayagyi said he got up at midnight and left the monastery through the eastern gate without disturbing anyone's sleep. So neither U Ko Lay (U Tejinda) nor U Hla Tun were aware that he went to the site where the Sayadaw's pagoda was to be built and sat on the precise spot and meditated. Then he recited the Parittas and Paṭṭhāna and returned to his quarters.

G. As I [Sayagyi U Chit Tin] happened to be close to Sayagyi after I started working in his office, I was aware through the officer responsible for the disbursement of salaries of all the officers and staff that Sayagyi did not handle his salary because he observed the ten precepts from the full-moon day of each month to the new-moon day. So that officer took his pay package directly to Sayagyi's family and Sayagyi never had to handle money. One reason his pay went directly to his family was that Sayagyi had eight children to support. He would have had nine children, but the first child died when she was very young.

Sayagyi held three or four separate posts (three posts for three years and four posts for one year) that were all equal to the rank of a head of department. The salary for each post would have been K 1,600, but Sayagyi was only allowed to draw a salary from one post (Director of Commerical Audit). All the other posts were only honorary. This clause was added to his appointment order, for otherwise he was entitled to draw K 300 for an additional post under the fundamental rules of the country. This clause in his appointment order took away his right to the extra pay. If he had been paid K 1,900 per month, he would have made more than his immediate superior, the Auditor General, who was paid only K 1,800 by virtue of his appointment through an act of parliament. Later, when Sayagyi was attached to the Auditor General's office as the Officer-in-charge on special duty, he prepared a very good case for increasing the Auditor General's salary to K 2,500 per month. This was approved and the act was amended. After that, Sayagyi could draw an extra K 300 for only one of his additional posts. He used this added sum for his personal expenditures. From his savings out of this additional salary, he gave *dāna* as part of his *kusala* actions.

Notes

Introduction

1. *The Path of Purification*, (Kandy: Buddhist Publication Society, 1975; 3rd ed., Shambala Publications, 1976).
2. "Webu Sayadaw" is a title meaning "the noble teacher from Webu." Though the title "Sayadaw" is used as a form of address without adding a proper name, every monk still keeps his monk's name, which in the case of Webu Sayadaw was Venerable Kumara.
3. For a description of the *dhutaṅga* (ascetic practices) see, Visuddhimagga, Chapter II.
4. A monk's requisites are: robes, alms food, shelter, medicine.
5. Sayagyi U Ba Khin, *Dhamma Texts*, 1985, p. 92.

Part I

1. The cycle of birth and death that is without discernible beginning, but which ends with the attainment of Nibbāna.
2. The Three Collections are the Vinaya-piṭaka or monastic discipline; the Sutta-piṭaka or book of discourses; and the Abhidhamma-piṭaka or philosophical treatises.
3. See Ven. Nyanatiloka, *Buddhist Dictionary* (Kandy: BPS, 1976) and Ven. Ledi Sayadaw, *The Manuals of Buddhism* (Rangoon, 1965), pp. 165ff.
4. For details, see p. 1.
5. *Citta* in Pāḷi means mind and mental functions. *Adhicitta* here means "concentrated mind," i.e., *samādhi*.
6. Matter, according to Buddhism, consists of subatomic particles (*kalāpas*) arising and disintegrating billions and billions of times in the wink of an eye.
7. *Kāya-pasāda* is the sensitive matter contained in the five physical sense organs that registers light (sight), sound waves, smells, tastes, and tactile sensations.
8. *Attā*, Pāḷi for "I," "soul," "personality," or any other type of permanent personal entity. Buddhism holds that such an entity does not exist and that the erroneous belief in a self is due to wishful thinking and wrong view of reality. See Saíyutta Nikāya, III 78, 196.
9. Sāsana (the teachings of the Buddha); there is a belief in Buddhist countries that the religion of Gotama Buddha will last five thousand years and then be lost.

10. The life span of human beings is believed to change according to the level of morality observed on the human plane. It ranges from an incalculable (*asaṅkheyya*) down to ten years. See: Dīgha Nikāya, III 81ff., and Ledi Sayadaw, *Manuals of Buddhism*, pp. 112f., 116f.
11. Greed (*lobha*), aversion (*dosa*), and delusion or illusion (*moha*) are the three root causes of all suffering. *Lobha* includes all degrees of wanting, looking forward to, desiring, lust, etc. *Dosa* includes all degrees of aversion from slight aversion to intense hatred. Fear is also part of *dosa* as it contains aversion against the thing feared. *Moha* means delusion about the nature of physical and mental states. When a person does away with *moha*, he recognizes that all states of body and mind are unsatisfactory, impermanent, and devoid of a self or soul.
12. Pagoda, dome-shaped religious monument. It usually contains either relics of a Buddha or a highly respected monk, or a Buddha statue, the holy scriptures or other holy objects. Most pagodas are solid structures and cannot be entered. They are symbols of the Buddha.
13. *Ficus religiosa*, the tree under which the Buddha attained Awakening.
14. Uposatha: There are four Uposatha days a month, using lunar months: full-moon, new-moon, and both half-moon days. On the Uposatha days Buddhists traditionally observe the eight precepts and go to the monasteries for meditation and to listen to religious discourses. In urban Burma, Sundays replace Uposatha days while in rural Burma, the lunar calendar is still in use.
15. Lake Anottata: a lake in the Himavant (Himalaya) region whose waters always remain cool.
16. The Dhamma, the Buddha's teaching, can be practiced only in some of the thirty-one planes of existence. In the ones below the human plane, beings in the hells suffer too intensely to be able to practice the teaching (even morality), those in the animal world do not possess the intelligence required to understand the teaching, while in some of the highest *brahmā* planes it is impossible to have contact with the lower planes and therefore it is impossible to receive the teaching. Buddhas always arise in the human plane.
17. *Ariyas*, people who have experienced Nibbāna, have only a limited number of lives remaining until they reach the end of all suffering.
18. *Iddhipda*: The root or basis of attaining completion or perfection. *Viriya* (effort): "A person with *viriya* is infused with the thought that the aim can be attained by energy and effort. He is not discouraged even though it is said to him that he must undergo great hardships. He is not discouraged even though he actually has to undergo great hardships. He is not discouraged even though it is said to him that he must put forth effort for many days, months, and years. He is not discouraged even though he actually has to put forth effort for such long periods" (Ledi Sayadaw, *The Manuals of Buddhism*, pp. 190f.).

19. *Samatha* (calm) is a synonym for *samādhi*. (See Dhammasaṅganī, I, 54).
20. See note 14.
21. The four postures are sitting, standing, lying down, and walking.
22. A reference to the Abhidhamma. These factors together make up what we normally call the mind.
23. The *Abhidhammattha-saṅgaha* is a condensed survey of the Abhidhamma. It was compiled by a monk named Anuruddha, who probably lived in Sri Lanka between the eighth and twelfth century C.E. It is widely studied in Burma by monks and lay people alike. There are several English translations among them, *Compendium of Philosophy* by U Shwe Zan Aung (first published by the Pali Text Society in 1910) and *A Manual of Abhidhamma* by Ven. Nārada (Buddhist Publication Society, third revised edition, 1975).
24. The Burmese language has a number of nouns and verbs that are used only by or in conjunction with monks. For the rice offered to monks, a different word is used than for the rice consumed by the laity. There are also special "monks' words" for eating, sleeping, coming, talking, etc. The cultured Burman not only uses these special words to show his respect when talking to a monk, he or she will also refer to himself or herself as "your disciple" and to the monk as "Lord."
25. Discourses about the Dhamma or the "Universal Law" as explained by the Buddha are given by monks to lay disciples on request. Monks normally give a Dhamma lecture after a meal offered to them, but there are also Dhamma lectures organized for big gatherings and given by famous monks.
26. *Akāliko*: one of the six qualities of the Buddha Dhamma. *Akāliko* literally translated means "no-time," immediate. One who practices the Buddha's teachings gets immediate results.
27. The sixth precept forbids the consumption of solid food including milk after twelve noon.
28. *Maggaṅga*. See Ledi Sayadaw, *The Manuals of Buddhism*, pp. 221ff.
29. *Bodhisatta* ("One who aspires to awakening"), a Buddha-to-be, is an individual who, inspired by a Buddha, takes a vow to work for the attainment of Buddhahood; "from then onwards, existence after existence, the Bodhisatta conserves mental energies of the highest order through the practice of the ten *pāramīs* (or Virtues towards Perfection)." (U Ba Khin, *What Buddhism Is* [Yangon 1954], p. 6). This reference is to Mahākapi-jātaka (Jātaka no. 516).
30. *The Path of Purification* (*Visuddhimagga*), I, 135.
31. Visākhā was an eminent female lay disciple of the Buddha. Anāthapiṇḍika was an eminent male lay disciple of the Buddha. For the story concerning him that Ven. Webu Sayadaw gives here, see *The Book of the Discipline*, V 216–23.

32. Cemeteries are believed to be infested with ghosts and ogres and other lowly beings. To be able to go through a cemetery one has to be either very courageous in a worldly sense, or have a mind developed in concentration and, if possible, insight (*paññā*). Persons of good morality and a developed mind are believed to be protected against mischievous lower beings. There is a meditation that is carried out in the cemetery to realize impermanence through the observation of decaying corpses. A person practicing this is highly admired and respected in Burma.
33. "The path and fruit of stream-entry," the first of the four stages towards Nibbāna.
34. One *asaṅkheyya* is equal to 1 followed by 140 zeros.
35. See note 21.
36. See note 18.
37. A Universal Monarch rules the whole planet righteously. Under the rule of the Universal Monarch there is prosperity and security for human beings. The Jewel of the Wheel, mentioned just below, arises when he has fulfilled all the conditions necessary to acquire this status. (See Dīgha Nikāya, III 81.)
38. *Pwe*, traditional Burmese theatre. It incorporates in a traditional play elements such as drama, clowns, music, dances, etc. It usually lasts all night until sunrise and the people eat and enjoy themselves. It is attended by the whole family, takes place on the village green or, in modern Burma, in town halls. The performing troupes tour Burma in the dry season.
39. In rural Burma people sleep on mats on the floor. Spreading a mat means getting ready to lie down.
40. One of thirteen *dhutaṅgas*, practices of great renunciation. The monk observing the sitter's practice never lies down. Disciples of Ven. Webu Sayadaw still keep this practice up. (For a description, see *The Path of Purification*, II, 73–76.)
41. The moral precepts when taken by lay disciples from a monk are always recited in Pāḷi. Ven. Webu Sayadaw treats this taking up of the sitter's practice as a taking up of moral precepts. Taking this vow in Pāḷi gives it weight.
42. The verses of this Therī are found in Elders' Verses II, 102–106. Her story is given in the commentary on the Therīgāthā (Thī-a, 95f.; *The Commentary on the Verses of the Therīs*, 126–32). Cf. the story of Bahuputtikā, *Buddhist Legends*, II 160f.
43. In the Abhidhamma the Buddha explains that the last thought process is responsible for the rebirth consciousness. If the last thought process is accompanied by good mental states, the being produced by it is a happy being; if it is accompanied by fear or greed or aversion, for example, a being in the lower planes will spring into existence as a result. There is no gap in time between the last mind-moment before death and the first mind-moment

of the rebirth. (See the references to *paṭisandhi*, *cuti*, and *citta* in the index to Pāḷi words in the *Compendium of Philosophy*.)

44. This discourse was given by the Webu Sayadaw on his second visit to the IMC in Yangon. He started travelling widely in Myanmar only after his first visit to the IMC in 1953.
45. See note 18.

Part II

1. See Kindred Sayings, I 283–87.
2. See the Bhūridatta Jātaka (Jātaka no. 543). In this life, the Bodhisatta was reborn as a *nāga* [a kind of dragon]. Wishing to escape from that world in the future, he kept the Observance Days (Uposatha) in the human plane. Through a series of unfortunate circumstances he was discovered by a brahman snake charmer and drugged and beaten until all his bones were broken. As he was observing the Uposatha with the strong determination to keep his mind free of desire, jealousy, intoxication, and anger, he did not react to the brahman's attacks. Having gained power over him, the snake charmer used him to earn his living in the towns and villages. After a while, the Bodhisatta was freed by one of his brothers, and the brahman became a leper.
3. See Kindred Sayings, I 293–95.
4. For the following story, see Buddhist Legends II 86–89.
5. For information about Asoka's younger brother Tissa-kumāra (later the monk Ekavihāriya), see under his name in *Dictionary of Pāḷi Proper Names*.
6. Jātaka no. 546. In this life, the Bodhisatta was of great wisdom. Four brahmans, led by Devinda, were wise men who advised the king. Out of jealousy, they tried to persuade King Videha not to listen to Mahosadha's advice.
7. Published in Ven. Webu Sayadaw, *The Essence of Buddha Dhamma*, Yangon: Sāsana Council Press, 1978.
8. Ibid.
9. Dated 19 January 1976. Translated by U Ko Lay.
10. For the story of Ven. Sāriputta and Ven. Assaji, see *The Book of the Discipline* IV, 52–54.

Part III

1. An example of this is found in the Dhammapada Commentary: Venerable Anuruddha (one of the disciples of the Buddha) admonishes his sister Rohinī, who suffers from a skin eruption, to do works of merit. She erects an assembly hall for the order of monks and serves the Buddha and his company of monks food in the hall. Through this meritorious deed her disease is cured.

See Dhammapada-aṭṭhakathā, III 295ff.; Burlingame, *Buddhist Legends* (Pali Text Society [PTS], London 1979), III, pp. 95, 96.

2. "Webu Sayadaw" is a title meaning "the noble teacher from Webu." Though the title "Sayadaw" is used as a form of address without adding a proper name, every monk still keeps his monk's name, which in the case of Webu Sayadaw was Venerable Kumāra.
3. See *Visuddhimagga*, Chapter II.
4. A monk's requisites are: robes, alms food, shelter, medicine.
5. See Comment B, pp. 152-153.
6. Another way to translate the last sentences would be: "There are many ways to interpret. Just be mindful." In the introduction to *The Basic Teachings of the Buddha and Their Correct Application*, Sayagyi invites comments and criticism, and at the end of the booklet, he announces that this Dhamma Yaung Chi booklet no. 1 will be followed by no. 2 in which he would publish the comments received and his elucidation of these comments. In his biography of Sayagyi (p. 215), U Ko Lay mentions that Sayagyi planned to continue these publications. Webu Sayadaw, however, was concerned that this would develop into controversy and take up much of Sayagyi's time—time that could otherwise be used to teach meditation. This is why the Sayadaw added the final sentence in his remarks. Sayagyi accepted the Sayadaw's advice and did not continue the series.
7. The building in a monastery compound used for ordinations and other formal meetings of the Saṅgha.
8. See Comment A, p. 152.
9. Ven. Webu Sayadaw sat facing the Shwedagon Pagoda as it could be seen through the southern door when it was left open. A marble statue of the Buddha was installed in the southern cell a year later.
10. See Comment C, pp. 145.
11. Names are given to novices and monks depending on the day of the week the candidate was born. Different letters of the alphabet are assigned to each day of the week and the name given must begin with one of the letters corresponding to the day of birth.
12. The difficult-to-attain state of being a monk.
13. In addition to recording the time according to a clock, the traditional way of telling time by measuring the shadow cast by the sun is used in ordinations whenever possible.
14. See Comment D, p. 145-146.
15. See Comment E, pp. 146.
16. See Comment F, p. 146.

17. *Chet-tho* in Burmese indicates the place where the umbilical cord is buried, hence "the birth place." *Shwe* means "golden."

18. *Sīla-shin.* The tradition of the ordination of women has been lost in Theravāda Buddhism, and, according to the view of the leading Burmese monks, it can be re-established only by a Buddha. This means that women who want to lead a religious life in Burma dress in certain colours, shave their heads, and live in communities where they observe the eight or the ten precepts.

19. See Comment G, pp. 146-147.

20. In 1965, the minimum wage for a labourer was 3.15 *kyats* (K) per day.

21. The opening three verses of the Udāna spoken by the Buddha after enjoying the bliss of liberation for seven days under the Bodhi tree. One verse each was spoken at the end of each of the three watches of the night. Translated by John D. Ireland, *The Udāna, Inspired Utterances of the Buddha* (Kandy: Buddhist Publication Society, 1990), pp. 11–13.

22. The Enumeration of the Conditions and the Analytical Exposition of the Conditions in the Paṭṭhāna (*Conditional Relations*).

23. "The recitation of the investigation of conditional relations."

24. Sammāparibbājaniya-sutta (Sutta-nipāta, vv. 359–375), Kalahavivāda-sutta (Sutta-nipāta, vv. 862–877), Mahāvyūha-sutta (Sutta-nipāta, vv. 895–914), Cūlavyūha-sutta (Sutta-nipāta, vv. 878–894), Tuvaṭaka-sutta (Sutta-nipāta, vv. 915–934), Purabheda-sutta (Sutta-nipāta, vv. 848–861). Translated by K.R. Norman, *The Group of Discourses* (Pali Text Society, 1984). For a discussion, see Sayagyi U Chit Tin, *The Great Occasion,* Dhammadāna Series 9.

25. Dhammapada, vv. 153–154.

26. See *The Second International Conference and Ordination in the Tradition of Sayagyi U Ba Khin, 1988–1989,* Dhammadāna Series 11, pp. 84f.

Pāli-English Glossary

Abhidhamma: ultimate truth. The Abhidhamma-piṭaka is the third section of the Buddhist canon.
Abhidhammattha-saṅgaha: an introduction to the Abhidhamma written by Anuruddha Thera
adhicitta: higher mentality or concentration
adhiṭṭhāna-pāramī: the perfection of determination
adhicitta: higher wisdom
adhisīla: higher morality
adosa: non-anger
agga-sāvaka: chief disciple
ājīva: livelihood
akāliko: immediate (see Part I, note 26)
akusala: unskilful
alobha: non-greed
amoha: non-delusion, knowledge, understanding
anāgāmī: non-returner
ānāpāna: meditation on the breath
Anuruddha: author of Abhidhammattha-saṅgaha
Anāthapiṇḍika: a leading lay disciple of the Buddha
anattā: non-self
anicca: impermanence
Anottata: a lake in the Himalayas whose waters always remain cool
āpo: water, the element of cohesion (one of the *mahābhūta*)
arahat: "Worthy One," a fully-awakened individual
ariya: "Noble One," an individual who has attained at least the first of the four stages along the path to Nibbāna
arūpa: immaterial
asaṅkheyya: incalculably large number
attā: self
aṭṭhakathā: commentary
avijjā: ignorance (of the Four Noble Truths)
avyākata: neutral action

bhāvanā: mental development
bhikkhu: Buddhist monk
bhikkhunī: Buddhist nun
Bimbisāra: king of Magadha and disciple of the Buddha
bodhi: awakening
bodhipakkhiya-dhammā: thirty-seven factors of awakening
Bodhisatta: "One intent on Awakening," Buddha-to-be
bodhiyaṅgaṇa: area around a Bodhi tree

brahmā: beings of the twenty highest planes of existence
brahman: member of the caste of priests in India
Buddha: "Awakened One"
Buddhaghosa: author of the *Visuddhimagga*

caraṇa: (right) conduct
cetiyaṅgaṇa: area around a pagoda
citta: mind
cuti: the last mind moment when "falling" away from a life (i.e., death)

deva: beings of the six planes above the human world
dāna-pāramī: the perfection of generosity
Dhamma: the teaching (of the Buddha)
Dhammapada: collection of verses spoken by the Buddha, part of the Tipiṭaka
dhutaṅga: ascetic practice
diṭṭhi: (right) view
dosa: dislike, aversion, hatred
dukkha: unsatisfactoriness, suffering

iddhipāda: "path to power" (see Part I, note 18)

Jetavana: monastery in Sāvatthī donated by Anāthapiṇðika
jhāna: absorption state

Kaccāna or *Kaccāyana*: a leading disciple of the Buddha
kalāpa: the smallest unit of matter (see Part I, note 6)
kāma: sensual desire
kamma: actions (the residual force of past actions)
kammanta: action
Kassapa: a leading disciple of the Buddha
kāyapasāda: clearness of the physical senses
khandha: aggregate
khanti-pāramī: the perfection of patience
kusala: skilful

lobha: wanting, greed
loka: world, sphere, a plane of existence

maggaṅga: the factors of the Noble Eightfold Path
magga: path
magga-phala: path and fruition state
mahā: great
mahā-bhūta: the "great" (primary) elements
Majjhima Nikāya: one of the four Nikāyas of the *sutta* section of the Tipiṭaka
mettā-pāramī: the perfection of loving kindness
moha: delusion

nāma: mind
nekkhamma-pāramī: the perfection of renunciation
Nibbāna: "quenching," the end of all suffering
nikāya: collections of *suttas*
nirodha: cessation

Pacceka Buddha: a non-teaching Buddha
pakati-sāvaka: an ordinary disciple (i.e., an Arahat, but not a chief disciple or leading disciple)
Pāḷi: the language in which the Theravāda Buddhist scriptures are written
pañca-sīla: the five moral precepts
paññā: insight, understanding
paramattha: highest, ultimate
pāramī: perfection
pariccheda (in *nāma-rūpa-pariccheda-ñāṇa*): the ability to distinguish between mental and physical phenomena
pariyatti: training (in the texts)
paṭhavī: earth, element of extension (one of the *mahā-bhūta*)
Pātimokkha: the collection of the 227 rules of conduct for the monks
paṭipatti: practice of the teachings
paṭisandhi: rebirth consciousness (following the last mind moment of the preceeding life, see *cuti*)
paṭivedha: attainment of Nibbāna
piṭaka: "basket," collection (of texts)
phala: fruition state

Rājagaha: a city in India
rūpa: matter

sacca-pāramī: the perfection of truth
sakadāgāmī: a once-returner
Sakka: the king of the *devas*
samādhi: concentration
samāpatti: attainment
samatha: calm
sammā: right, good
saísāra: the cycle of births and deaths
samudāya: origin [of suffering]
Saíyutta Nikāya: part of the Sutta-piṭaka
Saṅgha: the Order of Buddhist Monks
saṅgīti: Buddhist Council
saṅkappa: thought
saṅkhāra: the force of past actions
saññā: perception

Sāsana: the teachings of the Buddha
sati: attention, awareness
Sāvatthī: a city in India
sikkhā: training
sīla: morality
sotāpatti: stream-entry, first stage of Awakening
sutta: discourse
Sutta-piṭaka: the book of discourses

tejo: fire (one of the *mahā-bhūta*)
Thera: Elder (form of address for Buddhist monks who have been ordained for more than ten years)
Therī: corresponding form of address for Buddhist nuns
Tipiṭaka: the three collections (of the Pāḷi Canon)

upasampadā: ordination as a full member of the Saṅgha
upekkhā-pāramī: the perfection of equanimity
Uposatha: observance day (see Part II, note 14)

vācā: speech
vāyāma: effort
vāyo: wind, the element of motion (one of the *mahā-bhūta*)
vedanā: sensation, feeling
vijjā: understanding (of the Four Noble Truths)
Vinaya-piṭaka: book of monastic discipline
viññāṇa: consciousness
vipassanā: insight
viriya: effort
Vīsākhā: a leading woman lay disciple of the Buddha
Visuddhimagga: a general exposition on the teachings of the Buddha by Buddhaghosa

ABOUT PARIYATTI

Pariyatti is dedicated to providing affordable access to authentic teachings of the Buddha about the *Dhamma* theory (*pariyatti*) and practice (*paṭipatti*) of Vipassana meditation. A 501(c)(3) nonprofit charitable organization since 2002, Pariyatti is sustained by contributions from individuals who appreciate and want to share the incalculable value of the *Dhamma* teachings. We invite you to visit *www.pariyatti.org* to learn about our programs, services, and ways to support publishing and other undertakings.

Pariyatti Publishing Imprints

Vipassana Research Publications (focus on Vipassana as taught by S.N. Goenka in the tradition of Sayagyi U Ba Khin)

BPS Pariyatti Editions (selected titles from the Buddhist Publication Society, copublished by Pariyatti)

MPA Pariyatti Editions (selected titles from the Myanmar Pitaka Association, copublished by Pariyatti)

Pariyatti Digital Editions (audio and video titles, including discourses)

Pariyatti Press (classic titles returned to print and inspirational writing by contemporary authors)

Pariyatti enriches the world by

- disseminating the words of the Buddha,
- providing sustenance for the seeker's journey,
- illuminating the meditator's path.

Made in the USA
Las Vegas, NV
21 December 2023

83346916R00104